RICE

SPO

J. MOTTE ALSTON (1821–1909). PHOTOGRAPH FROM 1953 EDITION.

RICE PLANTER AND SPORTSMAN

The Recollections of J. Motte Alston, 1821–1909

EDITED BY ARNEY R. CHILDS
With a new introduction by Franklin Burroughs

UNIVERSITY OF SOUTH CAROLINA PRESS
Published in cooperation with the Institute for Southern Studies and the South Caroliniana Society of the University of South Carolina

SOUTHERN CLASSICS SERIES,
JOHN G. SPROAT, GENERAL EDITOR

The Georgetown County Historical Society donated funds to publish the illustrations in this volume. Its gift is in memory of George C. Rogers, Jr., historian of Georgetown County and of his native state.

Published in Columbia, South Carolina, by the
University of South Carolina Press in cooperation with the Institute for Southern Studies and the South Caroliniana Society of the University of South Carolina

Manufactured in the United States of America

03 02 01 00 99 5 4 3 2 1

Library of Congress Cataloging-in-Publication Data

Alston, Jacob Motte, 1821–1909.
Rice planter and sportsman : the recollections of J. Motte Alston, 1821 1909 / edited by Arney R. Childs : with a new introduction by Franklin Burroughs.
p. cm. (Southern classics series)
Originally published: 1953.
Includes index.
ISBN 1-57003-316-1 (pbk.)
1. Alston, Jacob Motte, 1821–1909. 2. Plantation owners—South Carolina—Biography. 3. Rice farmers—South Carolina—Biography. 4. South Carolina—Social life and customs. 5. Plantation life—South Carolina. 6. Outdoor life—South Carolina. 7. Georgetown County (S.C.)—Biography. I. Childs, Arney R. (Arney Robinson), b. 1890. II. Title. III. Series.
F274.A47 1999
975.7'03'092 dc—21
[B] 99-33521

To

Alice Ravenel Huger Smith

Who Has Helped to Keep Alive

The Spirit and Traditions

of Nineteenth-Century South Carolina

Contents

List of Illustrations ix
Series Editor's Preface xi
Introduction to the Southern Classics Edition xiii
Foreword xxxiii
Introduction xxxvii

1. A Tidewater Boyhood 3
2. The Bachelor Planter 41
3. The Sportsman 75
4. The Master of Woodbourne 102
5. The War Years and After 128

Genealogical Table 143
Index 145

Illustrations

J. Motte Alston (1821–1909), frontispiece

following page 74

The Waccamaw Neck

William Alston of Clifton (1757–1839)

Mrs. William Alston of Clifton (1769–1838)

Old Rice Mill at Fairfield Plantation

Motte Alston Read (1872–1920)

Series Editor's Preface

As THE opening sentence of *Rice Planter and Sportsman* indicates, J. Motte Alston wrote his recollections in the form of a letter to his grandson. His memoir thus affords intimate glimpses into the daily life of a lowcountry Carolina family, as well as commentary and opinion about such worldly matters as rice cultivation, slavery, and the sporting life. Franklin Burroughs's evocative and warmly personal introduction to this Southern Classic—a small gem of a lowcountry memoir in itself—notably enhances the appeal and value of these reminiscences.

Southern Classics returns to general circulation books of importance dealing with the history and culture of the American South. Sponsored by the Institute for Southern Studies and the South Caroliniana Society of the University of South Carolina, the series is advised by a board of distinguished scholars, whose members suggest titles and editors of individual volumes to the Series Editor and help to establish priorities in publication.

Chronological age alone does not determine a title's designation as a Southern Classic. The criteria include, as well, significance in contributing to a broad understanding of the region, timeliness in relation to events and moments of peculiar interest to the American South, usefulness in the classroom, and suitability for inclusion in personal and institutional collections on the region.

JOHN G. SPROAT
GENERAL EDITOR, *SOUTHERN CLASSICS SERIES*

Introduction to the Southern Classics Edition

FIRST HISTORY is shaped by landscapes, and then it overcomes them. So you drive the forty miles from Conway to Georgetown just as you drive any other forty miles of good paved road. The landscape demands no particular consideration; the layered, invisible past demands still less, even though the highway, this crossroads store, that cinder-block honky-tonk, and the tune and tenor of your own thinking are all incremental to it.

Approaching Yauhannah, Horry County slopes down to the Pee Dee floodplain, but the road continues on, straight as a surveyor's string, a high causeway carrying it across the swamps at almost treetop level. It rises for the Yauhannah bridge, and you look down at the Pee Dee, swirling and yellow brown with the clay silt of the Piedmont. Then you are over into Georgetown County, and a different past.

My father remembered a ferry at Yauhannah, before there was any bridge. He remembered an old road through the swamps, barely negotiable even in dry weather, that ran from the Conway-Georgetown highway down to Bull Creek. J. Motte Alston built that road, so that he could send a man up from Woodbourne every day, to meet the ferry and pick up his mail.

My own memory goes back only as far as a long, rickety wooden trestle—an elevated plank road—that preceded the present causeway. It seemed improvised and preliminary, like the scaffolding of a structure, not like the structure itself. The planks creaked and rattled under the tires. Every few hundred feet, the trestle widened, providing a place for one car to pull over when two cars met.

In my memory now, my father and I always cross at Yauhannah in predawn darkness. It is December or early January, and our destination is not Georgetown. A sudden fog surrounds us—the humidity of the swamps condensing in the cold, still night air. The guardrails on either side of the trestle are wooden slats, painted white. They reflect the headlights, vectoring two shining bands ahead of us, into a smoky oblivion of fog. When we go up over the bridge and come back down onto solidly grounded road in Georgetown County, it is like an airplane landing at night—a thump, a shudder, a safe reentry into a new place.

A bit farther down the highway is Plantersville—a big live oak hanging out over the road; a long, collapsed shed, half buried by wisteria. Here we turn left, onto a sand road. It runs through a country of longleaf pine ridges and slow, swampy creeks. Sooner or later—just this side of Chapel Creek or some distance beyond it—we turn left again, this time into a gated drive. We are in a tunnel of live oaks now, their trunks coming into the headlights in a long colonnade. Beneath them, something changes; we are entering a world that is gated off not only from the public road, but from the present. Your sense of yourself—of who you are, of how you should think and feel—grows slightly solemn, the way it does when you step inside a cathedral.

At the end of the drive a house looms up—Chicora Wood or Arundel or Springfield or Nightingale Hall. Beyond it lies the river itself, smaller here than back upstream at Yauhannah. And across the river is our destination, the marshes of the Pee Dee–Waccamaw delta that were and are still called the ricefields, although I have never met a single woman or man who had any memory of the time when rice actually grew in them.

Back in Horry County, when we went quail hunting on somebody's farm, we always stopped at the house, knocked, and asked permission. Courtesy required that, and the same courtesy required that the permission be granted. Courtesy disguises all sorts of differentials of power and status, and that was why it was important to learn its uses—so that everybody on both sides of the transaction could go on believing in democracy and equality, and that the respect it paid came back as self-respect.

This ricefield business was different. It was a private world, more exclusive than a country club. Access was by invitation only, and I did not understand the politics of invitations. My father did.

The men who issued the invitations were wealthy, but had an ambition that went beyond wealth and was detrimental to it. Sometimes, and in part, it might be an ambition for political ingratiation and connection. A genuine love for hunting and fishing was also part of it. But at the heart of it was the staking of a claim to a legacy, an augmenting of the idea of the self.

My father kept himself aloof from politics, detested pretension, and would not become an accessory to either. He thought that the present owed to the admirable parts of the past integrity, not imitation. I know that now because I came to know him closely. But at the time of the wooden trestle at Yauhannah, he was simply my father, a fact that was fated and unalterable. All I knew was that he did not do what I would have done—he did not accept any and all invitations to the ricefields. Our trips there, which would have been limited in any case, were further limited by calculations that were invisible to me, about realities that were also invisible. His wariness about those invitations reflected a dignity that ran deep, and lay close to what he was as a man. But I can now see that the layered past also influenced it: in it, you could see a good deal of the historical relation between our world, Horry County, and the enchanted, exclusive, and exclusionary world of the Georgetown County rice planters.

I guess we went down there hunting maybe two dozen times in the years of my growing up; I doubt our combined bag exceeded a dozen ducks. We also twice managed to get to North Inlet, J. Motte Alston's boyhood playground, and the finest playground, I think, that any boy could ask for. Getting there involved launching a boat through the surf at Pawley's Island and running down the coast, just beyond the breakers. It was a hairy trip and produced no fish either time. I have spent rather more time on Sandy Island, opposite the site of Woodbourne on Bull Creek, and on the dark, sluggish stream that runs up the middle of it. Once or twice, I was there at somebody's invitation; the other times, I was trespassing.

So that is about the extent of my qualifications to talk about J. Motte Alston's memoir—that I knocked around a little bit in places that he had as his birthright. I knew those places had a history. The plantation houses were its most visible evidence, and all the glamour, nostalgia, and vicarious pride of the antebellum mythos surrounded them. But it was the ricefields themselves that were most potent. As a boy, I did not know that they had once been swamps of cypress and gum like the ones I was familiar with, further upriver in Horry. I assumed they had always been marshes, and that for a while rice had been planted in them, and that now they were marsh again. I understood, vaguely, that the narrow ditches we paddled down, hoping to jump a mallard or a summerduck, had been dug by slaves. But what I always felt on those winter mornings was not their relatively recent domestication but a wildness that seemed augmented by an unimaginable antiquity, like Stonehenge. These were big, open spaces, with a great sweep of sky overhead; the horizon would be the silhouette of an old dike, a row of bare trees, moss-hung and desolate, posted along it like a skirmish line. Those dikes could have been an earthwork put there by some race that had died out before history even began, for a purpose too deep for us to fathom.

I was like a good many bookish children in that my fantasies and daydreams began with a setting, a geography. Hunting and fishing fed those fantasies and fed off them in almost the same way that reading did. I did not aspire to wealth or fame; I wanted to be indigenous to a landscape that would be like a book, a narrative of which I would be the protagonist. And the ricefields of Georgetown County, with the adjacent marshes of North Inlet, were for me the most recurrent dreamscape. I lived in Conway, but led an imaginary life across the Pee Dee and downstream from Bull Creek, and along Waccamaw Neck, which was in my time monopolized not by Alstons and Westons but by Baruchs and Vanderbilts.

There has been some writing about this world. In my teens, I came across the writings of Archibald Rutledge, who still lived down along the Santee, on a former rice plantation that had been in his family for generations, and who hunted and fished in that handsome country. The writings were full of adventures that ought to have appealed to me, but did not, and I did not read his stories over and over again, the way I read *In Our Time* or *All Quiet on the Western Front* or the hunting stories of Nash Buckingham. I do not know whether Rutledge disappointed me despite the fact that he seemed to live a life so close to the one I dreamed of, or because of it, or simply because he was not a very good writer.

Later, I came across the books written by Alston's cousin Elizabeth Alston Pringle—*A Woman Rice Planter* and *Chronicles of Chicora Wood.* Published in 1913 and 1922, these recount both her antebellum and her postbellum life at Chicora Wood, and they are deep and serious books—along with Mary Boykin Chesnut's diary, the only writings I know of by members of the South Carolina aristocracy that have a genuine distinction, one that reaches beyond the place and time they inhabited.

Still later came Charles Joyner's *Down by the Riverside,* a history that incorporates the memories of former slaves. The whole physical, financial, and political structure of the Alstons' world rested on these people as squarely as a house rests on its foundations, and Joyner's book preserves details and voices that the Alstons themselves would have considered beneath the dignity of history.

But at the end of the day, there seems to me still a haunting disparity. On the one hand, there is the great power of this landscape and of the past that created it; on the other, there is the literary evidence we have to go on. Slavery imposed silence on slaves, and denied them literate expression. Its impositions on slave owners were much more subtle, but can to some extent be inferred from such evidence as J. Motte Alston's *Rice Planter and Sportsman.*

CHRONOLOGY

> But I am ever and anon getting ahead of my simple story.
>
> When I made the promise to record some facts of family interest, I little dreamed I would be led to retrace so many joyful or weary steps that mark the mile stones in a man's long pilgrimage. But I made a beginning and unless I hasten on, the sunset of this life may overtake me and so I call a halt for weal or woe to this home-spun tale.

As Alston's valediction implies, his "simple story" often rambles away from a sequential and chronological structure, and it is not always easy to connect the *where* and the *when* of his life. The following chronology is often approximate with regard to date, but at least establishes sequence.

- *1821.* JMA is born, the only child of Thomas Pickney Alston (TPA) and Jane Judson Smith. It is not clear whether he was born in Charleston or on Waccamaw Neck. If at Waccamaw Neck, he probably first saw the light of day at Maryetta, directly across Winyah Bay from Georgetown.
- *1823.* JMA's mother dies. His paternal grandparents, William and Mary Brewton Motte Alston, take him to live at Fairfield, several miles upriver from Maryetta.
- *1825.* TPA marries Susan Smith, evidently without his father's approval. Over the next eighteen years, the couple will have nine children. JMA remains with his grandparents.
- *1826(?)–1828(?).* JMA begins school in Charleston, at a gram-

mar school associated with the College of Charleston. Because his grandparents continue to spend their winters at Fairfield, JMA boards in the house of the Reverend Jasper Adams, the president of the College of Charleston.

- *1828(?)–1837.* JMA continues his education in Charleston. Declining health has obliged his grandparents to leave Waccamaw Neck, and take up permanent residence in "the old Brewton-Motte-Alston-Pringle house, King Street near the South Battery," in Charleston. For JMA, this is a great improvement, enabling him to live with his surrogate parents again, instead of with the austere Reverend Adams. At some point not specified, JMA switches from the grammar school to a school run by a choleric Englishman, Christopher Coates, on Wentworth Street, in Charleston.
- *1837.* JMA is sent to St. Mary's, a Catholic college in Baltimore. He seems to like the college and begins to apply himself there, but his health is undermined by the cold.
- *1838.* Mary Brewton Motte Alston, JMA's beloved and doting grandmother, dies. Shortly after her death, JMA, in bad health, returns from Baltimore to Waccamaw Neck, and stays with his father at Maryetta.
- *1839.* JMA's grandfather, William Alston, dies.
- *1838–1840(?).* JMA spends two years recuperating on Waccamaw Neck and attends, as a boarding student, a small school somewhere in the vicinity of Murrell's Inlet. During this period, TPA sells Maryetta to his brother-in-law, A. P. Hayne, and purchases True Blue, adjacent to Weehawka, which upon the death of his father, in 1839, he has inherited.
- *1840.* JMA, restored to health, supervises the planting of TPA's rice crop at Weehawka and True Blue, while TPA summers in Virginia. JMA at this point lives in the old family summer house on Debordieu Island, at North Inlet and convenient to his father's ricefields.
- *1840 or 1841.* In the settling of William Alston's estate, TPA gains title to six hundred acres of uncleared swamp at the junction of Bull Creek and the Waccamaw River, in Horry County. He deeds this over to JMA, who intends to establish a plantation there, and who names his new property Woodbourne.
- *1843(?).* At about this time, TPA purchases a thousand acres

in Habersham County, Georgia, and builds a house there, intending to take up permanent residence in the mountains. He leaves JMA in charge of True Blue and Weehawka. By this time, JMA apparently has his own summer residence, which he calls Cottage by the Sea, on Pawley's Island, convenient to his father's ricelands.

- *1845(?).* TPA, finding Habersham County unsuitable in the winter, comes back to True Blue, and henceforth spends the cold months of the year there. JMA apparently remains in charge of the planting, and spends his summers at Cottage by the Sea. But with his father's large family once more occupying True Blue, JMA builds a rough winter residence, which he calls a shanty, at Woodbourne. It is on Bull Creek, about a mile and a half upstream from where his overseer and slaves are at work clearing the swamps for his new plantation.
- *1847.* On seventy-five roughly cleared acres, JMA raises his first rice crop at Woodbourne. In the fall, he travels to Habersham County to hunt with his father. There he meets and falls in love with Mary Ann Fitzsimons.
- *1848.* JMA marries Mary Ann Fitzsimons in February. They go to Waccamaw Neck in the spring, apparently spending their first year at True Blue and Pawley's.
- *1849.* A twelve-room house is now completed at Woodbourne, and 450 acres of riceland are cleared. JMA and his wife take up residence, and the first of their children is born. Over the seventeen years that remain to JMA and Mary, eight more children will be born to them.
- *185(?).* After what may have been only one or two years, or as many as four or five, JMA and his wife find the isolation of Woodbourne intolerable. He buys a hundred acres from Plowden Weston at Murrell's Inlet, and builds Sunnyside there.
- *1858(?).* JMA sells Woodbourne to Henry Buck, sells Sunnyside to his half brother, and takes his family to Columbia, severing his ties to Waccamaw Neck and to rice planting. His ninth and final child is born in Columbia in 1863. Mary Ann Fitzsimons dies in 1866.

Of the second half of his life, JMA says virtually nothing. The story he wanted to tell essentially ends with his departure from the ricefields in 1858. His granddaughter reports that after the war, he tried his hand at growing cotton in Georgia and failed, and eventually moved in with two of his daughters, who lived in Washington, D.C. He died there in 1909.

THE LOGIC OF LOCATION

> Opposite Georgetown across Winyah Bay lies Waccamaw Neck, a peninsula of some forty miles long by three wide. On the east is the Atlantic; on the west, the Waccamaw River; and beyond, running parallel to the Waccamaw, is the Peedee. All the alluvial land on both sides of these rivers [was] planted in rice for some thirty miles. These were the tidewater rice lands worth from $100.00 to $200.00 per acre, according to the proper "pitch of the tide"; that is, their relative freedom from salt-water lower down the river, and freshets higher up. These lands are flowed or dried, on high or low tide. Forty bushels of rough rice (rice threshed, but not pounded) is the average number of bushels per acre though I have made sixty-five bushels per acre.

The subtle gradient of elevation that determined the "pitch of the tide" was the geographical fact that shaped history. It made Georgetown County the fiefdom of some of the richest families in antebellum America, and underlay a civilization that bore a genuine resemblance to the hereditary aristocracies of Europe; and it made Horry County an undeveloped backwoods, a demi-frontier whose citizens were largely ignorant, uncouth, and, from the perspective of Waccamaw Neck, almost feral.

Obviously, the closer the ricefield to the sea, the greater the risk of saltwater incursions; the further upstream, the more frequent and more severe the risk of flooding. Fields located approximately in the middle of the thirty-mile stretch Alston describes would be the most secure and therefore the most valuable; they were in effect the home office, the center of the family business.

Alstons (spelling their names with one *l* or two, but all members of the same clan) had been on Waccamaw Neck since well before the Revolution. They cleared land, drained swamps, built stately houses, planted more and more rice, and bought more and more slaves. If the American republic had established titles of rank on the British model, JMA's grandfather would have been something like Sir William of

Waccamaw. Like the English aristocracy, the rice planters had a social world that was based primarily on class, not on neighborhood. Its center—its London, so to speak—was Charleston, fifty miles to the south. Regular visits there were for pleasure, but also for business: it was the financial and political point d'appui of the plantation economy.

When William Alston, JMA's grandfather, died, the first thing that his father, TPA, did was to sell Maryetta, which was dangerously far downstream. He did not sell it to just anyone. It went to A. P. Hayne, who was married to TPA's sister Elizabeth. Money from that sale probably helped him acquire True Blue, which was adjacent to Weehawka, left to him by his father. He moved his household there. Weehawka and True Blue lie about halfway between the upper and lower limits of rice cultivation. TPA had probably been managing the riceland there for some time before his father died; his father had, after all, spent the last decade of his life in Charleston. In changing his place of residence to True Blue, TPA confirmed his new elevation within the clan. In selling Maryetta to his sister's husband, he saw to it that the clan preserved its holdings in their entirety.

JMA's life appears to follow the same pattern. He was clearly attracted to the wilderness and remoteness—and the hunting and fishing—of Bull Creek and Horry County, and to the challenge of clearing new land and establishing a plantation higher upriver than any Alston had attempted. But it is also probable that he, like TPA, stood no chance of gaining title to lands that lay closer to the heart of the Alston empire until such time as he inherited them. And inheritance was by no means certain. TPA himself had been temporarily disinherited by his own father, because William did not approve of TPA's second wife. JMA says nothing about his own prospects for inheritance. He was the eldest son, and the fact that his father entrusted him with overseeing the crop at Weehawka and True Blue may suggest that he was being groomed for the day when he would assume title to those lands. On the other hand, his father's second family was large, and since JMA never mentions either his half siblings or their mother, it is possible that he disliked them, or vice versa. At the very least, TPA would have confronted an unusually difficult decision in bequeathing the lands that were both the central asset of his estate and the jewel in the crown of the family patrimony. JMA was his eldest son, and had faithfully—and, by his own account, successfully—looked after the whole complex business of running True Blue during TPA's extended sabbaticals from Waccamaw Neck. But JMA had not been raised in his household, and TPA had his own second family—four of whose nine children were boys—to see to.

I am inclined to think that JMA built the plantation at Woodbourne assuming that it would be to him what Maryetta had been to his father—a way station, which he would be able to turn over to one of his children or sell to one of his half siblings in the event that he was designated the heir of True Blue. I would further conjecture that his decision to leave the ricelands altogether may have involved a realization that his father was unlikely to will the prime land of True Blue and Weehawka to him.

Thus it appears that JMA's career as a planter approximated that of his father. Each man probably began learning the specific details of rice planting from a very early age. But being a rice planter involved a great deal more than planting rice; it involved running a large, complex enterprise. We may doubt that slavery was what planters so often claimed—a benevolent and paternalistic enterprise—but we cannot doubt that feeding, housing, clothing, supervising, disciplining, and otherwise attending to a hundred or more people, who could not be permitted to fend for themselves, required great administrative and organizational effort. The plantations produced most of their own food—they were, insofar as possible, self-sufficient units. Capital improvements, repairs, tending to livestock and machinery, were necessary and essentially incessant undertakings. (JMA estimates that at Fairfield, when he was growing up, no fewer than fifty slaves were carpenters.) In addition, there was the matter of assuming a place in society, which required the resources of a plantation—a house, slaves, lands for hunting, and the like—and not simply an income and a private residence. It was probably usual for the father to help the son, as TPA helped JMA, by giving him lands as a kind of advance on his inheritance, so that the son could set up on his own, and prepare for the larger responsibilities that would devolve upon him when and if he inherited the father's primary estate.

The logic of the location was also seasonal. From 1840 until he left Waccamaw Neck for good in 1858, JMA was actively involved in growing rice. Summers in the ricefields were hot and unhealthy. Insects were terrible, and during the periods when the rice was covered by shallow, stagnant water, the air was fetid. The great virtue of Waccamaw Neck was that the planters there could retreat to the beaches in the summer, and still be within a few miles of their fields. The old Alston beach house was on Debordieu Island, overlooking North Inlet. JMA spent his summers there until about 1841, when he built Cottage by the Sea, north of Debordieu at Pawley's Island.

Woodbourne was not on Waccamaw Neck, and its location was disadvantageous. It was not feasible to commute to it from Pawley's or Debordieu. Planters on the Pee Dee side had a summer community at Plantersville, which was a slightly higher and more salubrious spot than the ricefields, but it was no more convenient to Woodbourne than the seashore would have been. JMA's eventual building of Sunnyside, at Murrell's Inlet, seems to have been an attempt at compromise—a year-round house. But it proved unsatisfactory. The trip from it up to Woodbourne would have been a fairly difficult one, particularly on a falling tide or in time of freshet. And his family continued to retreat to Pawley's or the mountains during the summer.

JMA seems not to have owned a house in Charleston or a place in the mountains, but he had regular access to both. If he had lived out his life as a planter, he most probably would have followed the pattern of his father and his grandfather, and increasingly disengaged himself from Waccamaw Neck. Charleston was a second home for his entire class, and the mountains provided a complete escape from the discomforts and duties of the plantation. Many planters, like JMA's friend and neighbor Plowden Weston, went regularly to Europe, but JMA's own tastes and activities do not suggest that Europe would ever have particularly tempted him.

JMA's account of his career as a rice planter is thus full of arrivals and departures to and from Waccamaw Neck—his life was a surprisingly mobile one. In his prose, the departures were reluctant, the returns were sweet, and Waccamaw Neck was a kind of Eden, just as I had imagined it to be when I was growing up. But the actual details of his comings and goings suggest both how unpleasant a place a rice plantation was, even for its owner, during the summertime, and how a planter might very well grow restive under the constraints that were attached to ownership.

ALSTON THE WRITER

> The South was ever a book-reading, but *not* a book writing people, and thus so many facts of deep interest are unrecorded, and

> come down to future generations in the shape of tradition; whereas, at the North, every minute occurrence is jotted down, revised, and corrected according to circumstances.

You cannot quite tell whether Alston is bragging or complaining here. Reading was a gentlemanly activity, like drinking good claret. Writing, he implies, had something petty and pusillanimous about it—a jotting-down of minute occurrences, an altering of their details for ulterior motives. We cannot categorically say of any historical or social circumstance that it will or will not produce a significant literature—all of our generalizations are after the fact. But it does not seem to me surprising that the landed aristocracy that Alston epitomized gave so little account of itself.

It is essential for any hereditary social class to make its authority and entitlement seem inevitable, assured, undivided, and uniform. At least rhetorically, an allegiance to the past, to customary and undeviating procedures and strict regularity of conviction is necessary, to create the impression that the aristocrat is not imposing an arbitrary order by the strength of individual will and energy, but upholding an established, "natural" order, which assigns roles, obligations, and stations in life to all people. Introspection, the withdrawal into an idiosyncratic reality or a skeptical relation to received opinion, was at best a shirking of responsibility. The planter society in which Alston lived and moved was no more conducive to the production of literature, or even its serious discussion, than the upper echelons of the United States Army.

JMA ostensibly wrote only for his descendants, and did not foresee publication. But he had a high degree of literary self-consciousness. Here we are in Cooter Creek, on Sandy Island, fishing for bream: "Soon we reach the entrance of the long winding creek, where branches of living green dip nearly into the still water on either side, in which the finny beauties love to shelter themselves when the rays of the sun throw too much light on these shady surroundings. As we enter the lake to the left not a ripple disturbs its glasslike surface, over which dart, here and there, winged insects of various hues, at which ever and anon some greedy trout will strike." This has a somewhat labored elegance. "Ever and anon" is a genteel archaism; "finny beauties," "branches of living green," and "winged insects of various hues" fastidiously avoid anything resembling ordinary directness and simplicity of language. JMA's prose is full of descriptive set pieces like this, and they typically seem bent on translating his world into the stylized circumlocutions of eighteenth-century pastoral.

When JMA takes his catch back across Bull Creek to Woodbourne, helps us to sherry from the ancient sideboard, then serves the delicately fried fish to us in pairs, on covered plates, and follows them with some old cognac, we see a continuity between his manner of writing and his ideal of living. In each case, the substance is thoroughly local and indigenous; as if to compensate, the style is ostentatiously formal and elaborate. The authority of the author is not in the candor, conviction, freshness, or naturalness of his own voice, but in his fidelity to an imported and stately idiom.

From beginning to end, JMA's memoir is elegiac: he is writing about a lost past and a lost culture. It is also and inevitably polemical—a continuation of the lost war and an assertion of the lost cause by other means. The past is idealized and immobilized, because the idea of perfection has the idea of inherent immutability as its corollary. Nothing that we read in JMA's memoir prepares us for the moment when he sells off his holdings and voluntarily leaves the ricefields. We had naturally assumed that only the disasters of war, waiting in the wings, could sever his connection to his patrimony.

As we set the actual events of his life, as outlined in its chronology, against the tale he tells, we begin to sense that he practices what Edmund Burke calls an "economy with the truth." I do not wish to say that such economies are necessarily wrong; they may be quite justifiably mandated by a decent reticence, an unwillingness to wash dirty linen in public, and even by the requirements for coherence and consistency that are integral to writing.

But JMA's economies are excessive. He can admit no imperfection in the ethos and economy of the rice plantation, and therefore he can admit none in his own life. He quite naturally defends slavery—the more equivocal the basis of our own preeminence, the more strident our justification of it. His defense is not original; it closely resembles that of the antebellum Charleston lawyer William Grayson, in his long didactic poem, *The Hireling and the Slave.* Like Grayson, JMA celebrates the security, comfort, and happiness inherent in the unemancipated condition. Directly behind Grayson, and more distantly behind JMA, we see Pope's rationalization of the social order in *The Essay on Man:* human inequality reflects the hierarchical structure of the entire creation, which assigns masters responsibility for slaves and authority over them in precisely the way that it assigns parents responsibility and authority in relation to their children. In JMA's vision, life on Waccamaw Neck fuses nature and civilization, preserves unbroken all the sacred linkages of the chain of being, and in doing so, establishes a stable system of reciprocal fidelity and dependency. JMA insists that fear has no place on the plantations of Waccamaw Neck, despite the fact that the black population outnumbered the white by a ratio of at least ten to one: "a safer country could not be found. Crime was nearly unknown; petty thefts are all I remember."

But his own narrative provides evidence to the contrary. The fear manifested itself in the planters' persistent conviction that their slaves belonged to an essentially wild species, one that could be domesticated, and made useful and loyal, but that might at any moment revert to savagery. JMA heard tales of their cannibalistic propensities at his grandfather's knee (p. 49). At Woodbourne, his own devoted headman, Cudjo, was murdered by a less favored slave. The level of fear—and, with it, of coercion—underlying the Alston world is suggested by JMA's casual allusion to the penalty any white man or woman would incur for engaging in unauthorized barter, no matter how trivial, with slaves on another man's plantation: "whipping at the Cart's-tail on the public square of the district courthouse" (p. 55).

There is no reason to doubt that JMA's slaves were well cared for: they were extremely valuable. But, notwithstanding his professions of paternal solicitude, it is clear that they were at bottom a form of wealth. When he sold Woodbourne, he hired out all the hands who worked there to the new owner, Henry Buck, and thus continued to profit from slave labor while ridding himself of the responsibilities of ownership. His half brother Charles, in buying Sunnyside from JMA, used slaves—which TPA had given him—as partial payment. JMA then sold these to Governor John L. Manning, in Columbia, "except about thirty-five who had been in the family all their lives." These he "hired out to the railroad near Columbia," where, of course, they "seemed perfectly contented." In the last analysis, he treated his human property exactly as a stockbroker treats a share of stock—as an investment, a source of income, a commodity to be traded without sentimental compunction. In doing so, he was doing nothing reprehensible by the lights of his culture, and perhaps we cannot condemn him for being no better than his peers. But he in fact condemns himself, by his own rhetoric of loyalty and paternal responsibility.

JMA economizes the truth again in his depictions of family life, which is not to say that he dissimulates. What we get is something like a photograph album. We see scenes and occasions, people attractively posed, and we hear the anecdotes that attach to them. But for the Alstons, the family was more than a domestic affair. It was also a powerful economic consortium. The buying or selling of land and the building or leasing of houses, the management of each detail of the rice crop, the decision to marry, or to have children, or to summer in the mountains—none of these was merely a private, or merely an economic, decision. One would give a good deal to know the frictions and frustrations that were involved in being an Alston, as well as its amenities.

Occasionally, we get a glimpse behind the decorous facade: TPA's second marriage caused a temporary breach with his father; the partition, by lot, of ten thousand acres of land in Horry County between TPA and his two brothers was plainly a tense affair, upon which JMA's hopes depended; JMA's wife was unhappy at Woodbourne, and also unhappy at Sunnyside, which implies a marriage with at least its share of miseries. And domestic miseries radiated outward, into the intricate web of family connection and financial negotiation. JMA's decision to sell Woodbourne was taken without consultation and was quite sudden. That he sold it huggermugger to Henry Buck, a transplanted Yankee and an Horryite, with no connections to his family, cannot have pleased JMA's half siblings, his uncles, his in-laws, or his cousins. He was acting independently, alienating a portion of the family patrimony that his uncle William had particularly coveted; that act probably implied or occasioned some alienation of JMA himself from the extended family.

JMA was a child whose unruliness and strength of will were apparently fortified, not diminished, by the many thrashings he earned from his schoolmasters. His love for hunting and fishing and for the isolation of Woodbourne suggests a determination to do things on his own and in his own way, and supports the impression that he may have been something of a maverick within the Alston *gens*. But he writes—he *must* write—not as an individual but as an exemplar, a specimen of an ancien régime that history has repudiated. When a culture has been obliterated, it becomes sacrosanct among its survivors. The last great patrimony of the Alstons and the rice planters generally was nostalgia. And nostalgia, whatever else it may be, is always at least these two things: with respect to the past, it is a selective amnesia; with respect to the present, it is a sentimental repudiation.

He we are, back at Woodbourne, "one of the loneliest and most inaccessible places imaginable":

> This then was not an enchanting spot, but here we lived, cut off from the world, and yet how fondly does memory retrace its weary, care-laden steps and bask once more in the sunshine of so many happy hours, where
>
> "There is a society, where none intrudes . . ."
>
> The candles have just been lighted and a bright and cheerful wood fire helps to shed its influence on the lovely picture before me, as I stand at the door and gaze upon it. A beautiful young mother, sweetly dressed is seated near, while at her feet, on the rug, her little boy is playing with the folds of her gown. I have been on the lake duck-shooting and come in laden with beautiful green-head mallards and more beautiful wood-duck, and I draw the child away and surround him with the game and we clap our hands to see him try to embrace them all at once. Surely there was joy and untold happiness in that room which words could not describe, even though the tangled moss swayed to and fro from the gloomy cypress, and the huge horned owl, in melancholy tone, hooted to its mate across the river. The wild outlook was hidden from the happy hearts within, where cheerfulness smiled at the extreme gloom.

This, I realize, comes closer than anything else I have read to the world I dreamed of growing up: duck hunting as its primary activity; a house like a castle, safely cut off from the present and surrounded by wilderness; myself as the paterfamilias, the huntsman, and at the same time the child, whose initiation into the mystery of hunting still lay in the future. The ratifying and approving presence of a beautiful woman, and the surrounding swamps, with their lurking narratives of gothic adventure, make it complete and sufficient to all hungers of boyhood imagination.

I now sit a thousand miles from Bull Creek, the Waccamaw, Sandy Island, and all the rest of it. My experiences of those places were thirty-five and forty years ago. These things come between me and JMA's "lovely picture," and make me want to examine warily the invitation to fantasy that it extends.

It is another of JMA's set pieces, like a genre painting: The Hunter's Return. I look at Mary Ann Fitzsimons Alston, and think of her. Everything written on the subject, and details of JMA's own book, indicate that the wives of rice planters had responsibilities that were parallel to those of the planters themselves, and no less arduous. Further, we know that for virtually the whole of her married life, Mary was either pregnant or recovering from pregnancy: her children were born in 1849, 1850, 1852, 1853, 1855, 1857, 1859, 1861, and 1863, and she died three years later. It seems unlikely that many, if any, of the Alston children were born at Woodbourne. Mary surely would have gone to Waccamaw Neck, if not to Charleston, for her lying-in and her recuperation. Her life at Woodbourne was one of great fatigue, interruption, busyness, and anxiety, and we know that she was not happy there. She would have had small opportunity, and perhaps small inclination, to dress in her gown and serve as an accessory to a pile of mallards. But prosaic details—those "minute occurrences" so dear to Yankee writers—have no place in JMA's idyllic reverie. The story of a marriage that was, among other things, also shaped by the logic of location is a story veiled from us.

So JMA's way of writing removes incidents from the context of experience, freezes them in memory, and arranges them into tableaux like this one. Time, longing, the threat and temptation of change that are part of every human moment are banished. Or, rather, they are all deferred, as though only the Civil War brought them to the ricelands. He depicts an innocent world, and innocent worlds are axiomatically lost worlds. His aim as a writer was not to represent his world as belonging to the problematic condition of life, but to enshrine it as a sort of higher reality.

After a few more paragraphs of idealized description of life at Woodbourne, and a few digressive anecdotes triggered by them, JMA pulls us up short: "I have given thus far a picture of a planter's life in the low country of Carolina, and so I will not dwell much more on our life at Woodbourne, as it is becoming monotonous to anyone who should read these pages—so was it eminently so to me, to endure and enforce on one so dear to me, and the little group which had gathered about our knees."

This single brief paragraph gives us the consequences of circumstances that are never disclosed. The consequences are enough for us to know that, whether spoken or unspoken, inwardly acknowledged or inwardly denied, a consciousness of having inflicted suffering was a subtext of JMA's life at Woodbourne, and it ultimately led to his abandonment of what seems to have been not simply a patrimony, but a hereditary vocation.

Henry David Thoreau famously required of every writer, first or last, a "simple and sincere account of his own life, and not merely of what he has heard of other men's lives; some such account as he would send to his kindred from a distant land; for it he has lived sincerely, it must have been in a distant land to me." Any past—and particularly any antebellum past—is a distant land, and when the past is a local one, we feel a kinship with its inhabitants, and a hunger for its details. My quarrel with JMA is that I find him an inadequate correspondent, one who falls down, I strongly suspect, precisely in the territory of what Thoreau meant by sincerity. It is as though a kind of disingenuousness were woven into the texture of his prose, and perhaps into his life. And yet, of course, I would much rather have the book than not have it. It is a voice from the distant land; it reveals some things directly, and other things by inference only.

When I was growing up, the names of the plantations that lay down in the ricefield country were familiar to me before I ever started hunting there. Hunters tell stories to each other; fathers tell stories to sons. And the settings were very important to the stories. My father would come back well after dark. I would hear the truck pull into the driveway and greet him when he came in the kitchen door. Or, if it was that late, and I was already in bed, he would come back to my room. He would remove the ducks from the pouch of his hunting coat, spread out the coat, and lay the ducks out on it. Nothing I ever found under a tree on Christmas morning was so wonderful. I would admire the birds, and he would talk, and I would hear about Chicora Wood and the Beck Pond and the Halfmoon Pond, or about Arundel or Nightingale and jumpshooting in places like Guendalose Creek and Jericho Creek. Other hunters, friends of his, spoke with the same intimate familiarity about Hasty Point or Exchange, or recalled some grand trip, long ago, to Hobcaw Barony or Arcadia, where they had hobnobbed with exotic Yankee millionaires.

But I never heard of Woodbourne. And later, knocking around in that country, I never learned of its existence. The point of land formed between the north side of Bull Creek and the Waccamaw River, that looks across to Sandy Island and Georgetown County, is once more grown up in cypress and tupelo, not obviously distinguishable from any ordinary river swamp. The landscape here has swallowed history back into itself. For the staggering, savage labor of men working in muck and icy water and killing heat, making fields that were semifluvial, precarious, and lavishly productive of rice and money, there are no memorials, not even the silent, haunting evidence of dikes and ditches. The only evidence is JMA's book, his account of the place. If nothing else, the book is a document in the evolution of a specific nostalgia, the formation of an atmosphere composed about equally of yearning and forgetting, that still seems to hang like a mist over the places where J. Motte Alston lived the richest part of his life. In its mannered, provoking, and sometimes rather charming way, the book advertises that life. Caveat emptor.

FRANKLIN BURROUGHS

Bowdoin College

Foreword

THE REMINISCENCES of J. Motte Alston, from which the material for this book was drawn, are recorded in over five hundred large pages of closely written manuscript. There is an almost equally long supplement, written at another time, which was not used.

Some memoirs, officially not written for publication, seem, however, to have a mythical reader always in view; but not so in this case. Mr. Alston wrote as a labor of love for his grandson, who was keenly interested in family history in its personal aspects and in its larger integration with the history of South Carolina and the southern region. Mr. Alston obviously felt none of the restraint of other prospective readers and allowed himself the luxury of following a free range of thought, confident that his grandson would follow along with sympathetic understanding and supplementary personal knowledge.

The editorial task presented two problems: one of mechanical form and the other of orderly arrangement. Great liberties have been taken in conventionalizing Mr. Alston's punctuation and, in a few minor cases, modernizing his spelling and correcting obvious slips of the pen. The book is not burdened with indication of these alterations. The changes in organization have been more drastic: to the end that the reader may follow chronologically from childhood to old age, material has been brought together from widely scattered parts of the manuscript but not rewritten in the process. The words are Mr. Alston's own. All omissions and editorial interpolations have been indicated in the usual fashion. Footnoting has been held to a minimum and is designed to supplement and clarify the text for the reader, rather than to afford a checklist of the editor's familiarity with other sources. The genealogical table is not inclusive of all the ramifications of the four or five generations of Alstons before and after the author of these recollections. The Alstons were a prolific family; a complete genealogy would run to undue length and complexity. The simple form used in the appendix is chiefly concerned with the persons named in the book and the necessary connecting links. The index supplied is based on the theory that almost all books of any historical value should have indexes, and still serve their purpose.

As a study of rice planting in South Carolina, Mr. Alston's memoirs are not unique. The narrative is, however, clear, readable, and comprehensive. Beginning with the initial clearing of virgin land, discussing financing and marketing, as well as the detailed record of operation under ordinary and extraordinary circumstances, Mr. Alston livens his record with interesting anecdotes. He presents an unusually thoughtful analysis and a demonstration of the contrast between cotton and rice culture, pointing out that while continuous cotton planting exhausted the land the rice plantation had a new top soil each year. Starting from this simple fact he indicates other differences; the rice planter stayed in one place and kept his slaves with him, while the cotton farmer sought new lands and had less stability in his labor force. The cycle of work on a rice plantation called for a variety of tasks, some of them highly skilled. Therefore, Mr. Alston's head carpenter, Richmond, whose chief work was to see that the complicated machinery of the rice fields was in order as needed, could and did supervise the construction of his master's handsome twelve-room home. But even in this case, Richmond's plantation responsibility took precedence.

The South Carolina cotton planter seldom had use for more than a hundred slaves on a plantation in this state, the largest slave owners usually having lands "down the river" where the slave inventory might run into hundreds of names. On the other hand, Mr. Alston's grandfather, William Alston of Clifton, had between 500 and 1000 slaves, all of whom were on the Waccamaw River plantations owned by him or his sons. In this family situation apparently the ownership of the slaves was a matter of record, but the use was a matter of need. As a plantation passed from one to another member of the family it was not unusual to leave the slaves to their accustomed homes and ordered tasks. On the general relationship of master and slave (never called by that name) this record serves to enforce other accounts rather than make a new interpretation.

It seems unlikely that any cotton plantation in South Carolina involving a comparable investment was as lucrative as Mr. Alston's rice plantation proved to be in the period of his independent venture from 1848 to 1860. Little wonder that in commenting on the fact that he had lost a cotton farm because of neglect in recording of the deed

Mr. Alston said, "but then, the Alstons never though much of cotton land."

To some readers, Mr. Alston's experiences as a sportsman will be the most interesting part of this book, although nostalgia for those days of the abundance of fish and game in the South Carolina Low Country and the Blue Ridge Mountains will surely follow. Other readers, less interested in gun and rod, will note the range of Mr. Alston's knowledge of bird life, or be moved by his sensitive response to the varied beauty of his surroundings.

It may be interesting to note that much of the land over which Mr. Alston hunted with such avidity and success is now in privately owned game preserves. As one rides today along the highway which cuts through the old Alston plantations that in Motte Alson's time ran from river to sea coast, one sometimes sees deer among the great old trees which are still hung with the grey moss so distinctive of the Low Country.

The editor leaves daily contact with the memoirs with a sense of personal loss. The chief interest centers around the character of the author: his high principles, his delightful humor, his accurate observations, the thoughtful analysis of his time, and the warm human relationships. The book is published with the hope that the savor of the man and his day will be caught by the interested and sympathetic reader.

A. R. C.

Introduction

J. Motte Alston, my maternal grandfather, was an intimate part of the first thirty years of my life, and, by a strange act of destiny, I was the person to open and read the manuscript he published.

Written in his latter years at the request of my brother, Motte Alston Read, his namesake and eldest grandchild, it was sealed and put away, in accordance with his instructions that it was not to be opened for twenty-five years. The passing of those years took the lives not only of my brother, who had lived in Charleston after his resignation as Assistant Professor at Harvard College on account of ill health, but of all those who would have been interested in his reminiscences from a family viewpoint. It was, therefore, my sad duty to open, read, and then put away the manuscript with no thought of publication. Last year it was read by friends in Charleston who thought that his informal narrative, written about the life and history of rice culture in South Carolina at the peak of its prosperity, would be of sufficient interest to preserve in published form. With this in mind, I take great pleasure in adding some biographical data and stories which I, as a child, delighted in hearing.

During my first reading, trying to decipher a beautiful but most difficult hand-writing, I recalled the story of my grandfather sending a note to his overseer by his butler, Billy, only to have it returned by the same hand, with the remark: "Massa, he say he can't read one word you have wrote. How can you 'spec po' white trash like dat to read Gentleman's handwriting like yours?"

Pedigrees are boring, but blood lines important, so I will give briefly the background of the Alston family. John Alston was believed to be one of the Monmouth exiles who was banished from England in 1685. He was sent to Barbados, from there came to South Carolina, and settled in St. John's Berkeley. His son, William, married Esther Marboeuf, a Hugenot, and moved to All Saints Parish on the Waccamaw in 1730.

The first Alston plantation was The Oaks, where the old family graveyard—"God's Acre"—enclosed by a brick wall and iron gates, is still preserved. In this graveyard is buried Burr Allston, only child of Governor Joseph Allston and his wife, Theodosia, daughter of Aaron Burr. It was after the death of her son that she made the ill-fated voyage to visit her father from which she never returned. The vessel was lost, but there is no proof as to whether it was shipwrecked, or captured by pirates, and the passengers made to "walk the plank."

From this original settlement, various members of Alstons and Allstons expanded their vast rice plantations, so that most of the land from the top of Winyah Bay to the Horry County line was at one time owned by members of this family or the families with whom they had intermarried.

Farther down was Clifton, the home of Colonel William Alston, and it was with him that my grandfather lived during his childhood and boyhood, his mother having died when he was two years old. She was Jane Ladson (daughter of John Rutledge Smith, who was descended from Thomas Smith, first Landgrave of South Carolina). During these years when he lived with his grandfather, his attachment for the Low Country of South Carolina was first formed, and it was to this country that he returned when he was taken ill at St. Mary's College in Baltimore. His life on the Waccamaw River is told in the following pages, so I pass to my association with him in his later years.

My mother, Jane Ladson, was the third in a family of nine children of J. Motte Alston and Mary Ann Fitzsimons. She was only twelve years old when her mother died at the close of the War Between the States, but assumed the care of the younger children, and at nineteen was married to my father, William Melvin Read of Virginia. It was with them that my grandfather passed his winters at this period of his life, and that my association with him first come to my memory. During these long visits when my brothers were at school or Harvard College, I was my grandfather's frequent audience, when his memory went back to the happy past which so soon merged into the tragedy of the consequences of the War of 1861. Brought up as he was by his Grandmother Mary Motte Alston, there was perhaps an added interest to him in talking to *his* Granddaughter Mary, and to me it gave a vital, vivid interest, which had lasted all of my life, in the colonial years of this country. Mary Motte, daughter of Rebecca Motte of Revolutionary prominence, was one of the three daughters locked in the attic of the Miles Brewton house, 27 King Street, Charleston, while her mother presided at the dinner table when the British officers occupied her residence during the Revolutionary War. This war has, in consequence, always seemed close to me, from grandmother to grandson, grandfather to granddaughter.

On my first visit to Charleston as a girl, my grandfather was with us, and this old family house where he had passed a part of each year as a boy became a reality to me. To be taken to various nooks and corners of the old garden where his rabbits and pigeons had been kept is a charming memory.

It was many years later that I first visited the older homes of the Alstons on the Waccamaw, staying at Fairfield, the plantation next to Clifton, both of which are now the property of Mr. George Vanderbilt. I was the guest of my cousins, Mr. and Mrs. John E. Allston, and at this time the trip, even by motor, took almost a day because the bridge over the Cooper River was not completed. The old ferries over the North and South Santee rivers were still operated by Negroes who pulled a flat, on which your motor or carriage was put across the river by means of ropes; the same method which was used when General Washington visited Colonel William Alston at Clifton. I was driven on the old road known as the King's Highway up the neck to Brookgreen, the home of Washington Allston, the artist, which has since been purchased by Mr. Archer M. Huntington, who has restored the garden, placing in it the fine sculpture done by his wife and other artists. It has been given to the State of South Carolina.

During my visit to Fairfield, my hostess came to me one afternoon saying that Robert, an old Negro who had worked for my grandfather, had come to see me. I shall never forget this superb old man, white-haired, erect, who pulled his forelock in the old sign of *fealty,* saying: "Good evenin', Miss. I'se glad to see one of de Blood; I'se tired working for de Millionaries."

At that time game was still abundant, my host saying he was going out to "shoot our dinner, and what would you like?" "Green-wing teal," was my answer; and green-wing teal we had. At the time of my visit, the old rice fields and rice mills were still there but no cultivation, the country having largely become a game reserve for persons able to own and keep uncultivated lands for that purpose.

Before we leave the rice fields, it may be interesting to the modern housewife to read in the vernacular the pre-War directions for cooking rice given by a Queen of a Santee kitchen: "Wash the rice well in *two* waters, if you don't wash 'em, 'e will *clag* [clag means get sticky] and put 'em in a pot of well-salted boiling water. You musn't hab a heavy han' like'e was 'tata [potato] or sich, but *must* stir 'em in light and *generous* so 'e can feel de water all t'rou. . . When 'e done be sure you dish 'em in a hot dish les 'e take a smart chill and go flat."

My grandfather alludes only briefly to the years when he struggled to readjust his life and tried to grow cotton in Georgia, but as there was no similarity between rice planting and growing cotton, it was a dismal failure; so after a few years, he moved to Washington, D.C. where he lived with his two youngest daughters, Mary Alston, and Hesse, afterwards Mrs. Richard S. Trapier.

It was there that he passed the last years of his varied life, an onlooker, always amused and interested in the passing show, in what was fast becoming one of the great capitals of the world. A thin, erect old South Carolinian with white hair, pointed beard, moustache, in his tiny number five boots, he was a well-known private figure.

One day a much younger man stopped him on Connecticut Avenue saying, "Colonel Alston, I beg your pardon, but knowing you well by sight I would like to introduce myself and ask you a question: how have you attained your age with such perfect preservation of all your faculties?"

In recounting the incident to us, he remarked: "I thought the fellow was d——d impertinent but I told him the truth."

"What was that, Grandfather?"

His answer: "I have always observed moderation in all things, even to drinking water and saying my prayers!"

These prayers were often of his own composition and very beautiful, for he had the faith of a child which upheld him through a long and varied life which spanned one of the most critical eras of our country.

MARY ALSTON READ SIMMS

RICE PLANTER

AND

SPORTSMAN

1

A Tidewater Boyhood

YOU REQUESTED, some months since, that I would trace on paper such anecdotes, incidents, and scraps of family history, I may have remembered to have occurred, or to have been told me in the long ago.[1] These may prove of but little interest, nor will they be another form of the "Tales of a Grandfather"; but on the other hand, some little incidents here jotted down might prove of worth when you desire to turn back the pages of time and learn something of the home life of some of your ancestors; how, when and where they lived; what were their occupations, their manner of living, amusements, pastimes. Now I only exact one promise of you—that you will only look upon the personal pronoun "I" as simply the little instrument to record, and not the compound "myself," so self-sufficient and egotistical. . . . In all your researches for antediluvian remains, though you have looked much deeper than where our forefathers lie, still it may be of interest to you to bring to the light of day specimens which have been so long buried out of sight; as it will be for me to unfold the Manuscripts of Time and tell you something about them. . . .[2]

Like "Jacob Faithful I was not born on the angry ocean" but in full view of the same. On Norse blue waves our ancestors sailed into the then little settlement of Charles Town, between the Cooper and Ashley Rivers. This was a while before my day, but not before the

---

[1] These reminiscenses, written during the 1890's, are in the form of a letter from J. Motte Alston to his grandson, Motte Alston Read. The latter, son of Jane Ladson Alston and William Melvin Read of Virginia, was born June 20, 1872, and died July 12, 1920. See obituary notice in *The South Carolina Historical and Genealogical Magazine,* XXI, 136-37.

[2] Mr. Alston here had reference to his grandson's scientific training in paleontology and in other branches of natural history. Mr. Read was also deeply interested in history and genealogy. See *ibid.*

stately Saint Michael's was called the "New Church" for the reason that Saint Philip's antedated it; and the earthworks from one side to the other, called the "lines," built to protect the town from the Indians and subsequently from the English, had been wholly removed. . . .

The Alstons were English; the Mottes (De-la-Motte), Huguenots; the Smiths (Landgraves), English; and the Rutledges, Scotch-Irish. . . . We read of John Allston, and Arthur Middleton, political exiles, who, having sailed from the West Indies, landed in South Carolina where they remained. You perceive that the "Alston" is sometimes written "Allston." I remember asking my Grandfather, Colonel William Alston of Clifton, Waccamaw, South Carolina, why some of the family spelled the name with a double ell. I was a little fellow and spelling was a high art from my standpoint, and as my Grandfather was considered high authority, I applied to him. I well remember his reply, "The schoolmaster was not abroad in those days, my boy, and names were spelled as pronounced in this Country, and so Alston had two ells inserted." . . . You notice also that Washington Allston has two ells. His father was called "Gentleman William"; and my Grandfather, "King William" from his wealth and influence. . . .[3] My grandfather was as generous a man as ever lived; was fond of social life; devoted to politics and was a member of the legislature and State Senator almost as long as I can remember; Colonel of Militia; temporary editor of the Georgetown paper during Nullification days; an ardent sportsman and remarkably fine shot; fond of dinner parties, of which he was the very life; devoted to books and beloved by all; but he was careless about business matters—the very reverse of his father and his brother Charles, who were thorough business men. . . . William Alston married Mary Brewton, youngest daughter of Rebecca Motte of

---

[3] A further explanation of the spelling of *Alston* may be quoted from Elizabeth Deas Allston, *Allstons and Alstons of Waccamaw* (Charleston, 1936), p. 7: "The family of Alston in England from which the Waccamaw Alstons are descended generally spelled the name with one L, but the immigrant, John, added the second L to the name in his will, and it was spelled Allston by all branches of the family until William of Clifton, his great grandson, reverted to the old English way of spelling it. He and his father's first cousin, William of Brookgreen, both had the name of William, lived in the same part of the country and served as captains under Gen. Francis Marion . . . and as there was frequent confusion as to their identity, William of Clifton took this means of avoiding further trouble. So the descendents of William Alston of Clifton have spelled their name *Alston*."

the Revolution.[4] We won't go over the old story of the burning of her home on the Congaree River, twenty miles below Columbia.[5] . . . The portrait of Rebecca Motte, from which so many copies and photographs have been taken, was really not that of Rebecca Motte. I know that I am the only one living who knows this. I well remember saying to my father that the likeness of my great-grand-mother showed her to be a very masculine woman. He laughed, and told me that once, when on a visit to Cousin Thomas Pinckney, son of General Pinckney,[6] he asked him whose portrait was that, pointing to the one which has been assigned to Rebecca Motte. He laughingly replied, "I really do not know where that portrait came from, but I amuse people by telling them that it is my Grand-mother Motte, as it is so totally unlike her—she being frail and delicate and the portrait being just the reverse." This anecdote will give you a faint idea of "the truth of history." . . .

The Alstons were planters on the Waccamaw river, near Georgetown, South Carolina, a town settled in 1720, or '21. (This date may not be accurate and is given for what it is worth.) [7] It was never much of a town in spite of its royal claims, though at one time it boasted of a very refined society and your *Life of Marion* will tell you of the many acts of bravery around the old place by "Marion's Men." After the introduction of rice it became very unhealthy; and although on Winyah Bay—into which emptied the Peedee, Waccamaw, Black, and Sampit rivers—the intricate bar prevented its being much of a sea-port, and its unhealthfulness, a place of residence. I remember while living on Debordieu Island [8] during my juvenile

[4] A letter dated August 13, 1802, from Thomas Pinckney, Jr., to his daughter refers to Mr. and Mrs. William Alston in these words: "My Aunt Alston you know is at the Springs up the North River. I am glad she has influence enough with her precious helpmate to induce him to stay so long, so far North. His plan, you know, was to go immediately from here to Virginia, to be in the neighborhood of Race-horses and Democrats, two species of animals, you know, [of which] he is very fond." *The South Carolina Historical and Genealogical Magazine*, XLI, 115.

[5] See D. D. Wallace, *South Carolina: A Short History* (Chapel Hill, N.C., 1951), p. 316.

[6] For the Pinckneys see *Dictionary of American Biography*, XIV, 617-18.

[7] Wallace gives the date as 1729. See *South Carolina: A Short History*, p. 60.

[8] This word is variously spelled, though Mr. Alston usually uses the form recorded here. Henry D. Bull in *All Saint's Parish* (Charleston, 1948), p. 53, spells it *Dubordieu*. In *The South Carolina Historical and Genealogical Magazine*, XXVI, 156, and XXXIX, 126, reference is made to a Georgetown family of "Dubourdieu" for whom the island presumably was named.

days, the first question asked of one who had visited Georgetown in the sickly months of August and September was "who was dead?" This was before the days of quinine, when the lancet and calomel sent thousands over the "dark river" long before their time. If one had what was commonly known as "country fever," which was only a high grade of bilious fever, and a doctor was sent for, it was expected, so as to avoid delay, that bandages and a basin should be in readiness for the blood letting, and calomel was sure to follow; and if by good luck the fever was run out of the system by this heroic treatment, then tumblers full of Peruvian bark [were] administered to fill up the vacuum. The patient had now escaped a summer funeral "by the skin of his teeth," but dropsy and pleurisy from his depleted condition generally gave him a winter one. . . .

Opposite Georgetown across Winyah Bay lies Waccamaw Neck, a peninsula of some forty miles long by three wide. On the east is the Atlantic; on the west, the Waccamaw river; and beyond, running parallel to the Waccamaw, is the Peedee. All the alluvial land on both sides of these rivers [was] planted in rice for some thirty miles. These were the tidewater rice lands worth from $100.00 to $200.00 per acre, according to the proper "pitch of the tide"; that is, their relative freedom from salt-water lower down the river, and freshets higher up. These lands are flowed or dried, on high or low tide. Forty bushels of rough rice (rice threshed, but not pounded) is the average number of bushels per acre though I have made sixty-five bushels per acre on 600 acres of land. Rice is called "rough" unpounded, and "clean" when pounded or prepared for use. If you will examine Mills' *Atlas* . . . you will find the name of the owners of all the plantations on the Waccamaw River, and you will see the number owned by my Grandfather, Colonel William Alston and his sons.[9] He owned about one thousand negroes—we never called them "slaves," for really there were, and are more slaves among those called "free,"

[9] Robert Mills, *Atlas of the State of South Carolina, Facsimile Edition of the Original Published in 1825* (Columbia, 1937), shows sixteen Allstons (all spelled thus) on Waccamaw Neck between Winyah Bay and Bull Island. The name also occurs frequently on the Black and Peedee rivers and along the coast. At one sea-island location the name is spelled Alston. It seems clear that Mills did not use the distinctive spelling followed by the family and that the plantations located in the *Atlas* were owned by both branches of the family —not exclusively, as the text seems to indicate, by "William Alston and his sons."

than existed on well regulated estates owned by humane and intelligent and highly educated men and women.

Opposite Georgetown is Waccamaw, where the Alstons and many others lived in the winter months on their rice plantations. Here were many very elegant country homes; Clifton, the home of my Grandfather and Prospect Hill, that of his brother Thomas, were by far the handsomest.[10] Clifton was where my grandfather entertained President George Washington on his visit to Carolina. . . . He remarked, when standing on the piazza overlooking the Waccamaw and Peedee rivers, where thousands of acres of green rice-fields [were] in full view, and Georgetown and the old red-topped fort in the distance, that he felt as if in fairie land.[11] The citizens gave him a large ball in Georgetown, and I remember asking my Grand-mother, from whose dear lips I heard so many incidents, how she was dressed; and her telling me, first, a band on her forehead on which was engraved, "Hail to the Chief." This so captivated my childish fancy that the rest of her attire I took but little interest in.

Now, before I go any further, let me say, that a more lovely woman never lived than Mary Brewton Motte Alston. The miniature on ivory, painted by Sargeant of Philadelphia after the original by Charles Fraser of Charleston, South Carolina, will tell you how she looked when I knew her.[12] You know my mother died when I was just two years and two days old; and from that time till I went to Saint Mary's College, Baltimore, at the age of sixteen, I lived with my grandparents. Of course I made long visits to my father after his second marriage; but my *home* was where my beloved grandmother was, either in Charleston in the old Brewton-Motte-Alston-Pringle house, King Street near the South Battery, of which I will write more fully further on, or at Fairfield on Waccamaw, where my grandfather lived after the Clifton mansion was destroyed by fire.[13]

---

[10] Clifton and Prospect Hill are now owned by George Vanderbilt, whose residence is on the site of Prospect Hill. The Vanderbilt estate, now known as "Arcadia," comprises about 20,000 acres, including the plantations mentioned above, six other plantations, and Debordieu Beach. *The State* (Columbia), April 5, 1953.

[11] Archibald Henderson, *Washington's Southern Tour* (Boston and New York, 1923), p. 126.

[12] See reproduction in this volume. See also Alice R. H. Smith and D. E. Huger Smith, *Charles Fraser* (New York, 1924), p. 8 (reproduction of portrait) and p. 40 (description).

[13] Fairfield is described by Elizabeth Deas Allston in *Allstons and Alstons of Waccamaw*, pp. 25-26. Although the statement is there made that Fairfield was still owned by a member of the family, it is now a part of Arcadia.

Her [Mrs. Alston's] whole life was spent in doing good. Her means, of course, were ample, and to give money was an easy thing to do, but this was not the charity which lived in her noble heart. . . . Well do I remember the large mugs of tea and coffee with bread on the top of each she would fix with her own hands, after the family had finished breakfast, and send to the needy in the neighborhood. . . . Every day the carriage was at the door with the beautiful bay horses, and so often would you see the same at some fashionable store on King Street; and passers-by may well have thought how many purchases were being made; but she was not even in the stores; but would leave her carriage there, and on foot would wend her way to the homes of the poor and suffering, and so spend her money for the relief of the distressed; and it was only after her death that the family knew of her well-kept secret, by the poor who came to her door to pay a last tribute to her open handed charity. . . .

The rice-planters of Waccamaw would spend their winters on their plantations and their summers on the sea-islands near by. A chain of these islands extends along the southern coast. Sometimes you find them densely wooded, live-oaks and magnolias, and a number of other trees. . . . Some of these islands are only high hills of sand covered with a coarse grass indigenous to the coast. Debordieu, named after an old Frenchman who first lived there, was an island of this description. It was here that my grandfather lived in summer. His house was built to stand the hurricanes which would now and then sweep the southern coast. An under-ground frame of heavy timber on which the house was built has protected it from the winds and waves of a century, for the old residence is still occupied in summer by some of his grandsons. The great storm of October, 1822, which caused such destruction of life and property, did not injure this house. My father and mother and . . . [I], then only eight months of age, happened to spend the night here [at Grandfather's]. I have been told that it was a beautiful evening in October. . . . The hurricane occurred during the night and the sun rose next day in all its splendor, only to reveal the fearful destruction. My father's [own] house was ruined and the Meyers family were all drowned, their house having floated out to sea. One of my father's servants, Carolina, his cook, escaped from the falling building, and true to his calling appeared the next day with a pair of ducks which he had saved for dinner. . . . It was here I passed very many summers as a boy, shooting and fishing.[14]

It was here that Aaron Burr Alston died, at the age of twelve, the only child of Joseph and Theodosia. He was a wonderfully bright boy, and his death blighted his mother's life and caused her untimely end. She was devoted to her father, and he was equally so to her. It was during the war of '12 and she desired to go to her father in New York. Joseph Alston was then Governor of South Carolina, and by the laws of the State he could not leave Carolina. He had a pilot boat fitted out to take her North, and with her servants she sailed on her ill-fated voyage. The boat was laden with casks of rice to defray her expenses, and a letter was written to the British Admiral, off the Capes, advising who she was, and requesting permission for a passage through the fleet. This was all that was known during the life of her husband. He died about two years after she had sailed. Shortly after his death a member of the family traveling in England met the Admiral who had commanded the fleet, and he mentioned that the pilot boat had appeared, and that he had granted the request to allow Mrs. Alston to proceed to New York, but that same night a violent storm arose which scattered the fleet, which was all the light he could throw on the subject. He presumed that the boat went down with all on board.

This was all that was known of poor Thedosia's life about the year 1876. Every year, or two, newspaper accounts would appear; "Confessions of a pirate who had seen her made to walk the plank from some piratical craft" and full descriptions of her beauty. I remember having read many such. About the year above mentioned (1876), my Aunt Hesse[15] . . . received a letter from a gentleman, well known in New York, telling her that he possessed a portrait which was the counterpart of one in that city of Theodosia, the daughter of Aaron Burr and wife of Joseph Alston. This portrait had been left him by a friend, to whom it had been given by a physician who had practiced his profession on the coast of North Carolina years ago

[14] The storm of 1822 is described in Elizabeth Deas Allston, *Allstons and Alstons of Waccamaw,* p. 67. The seaside summer resorts of the Waccamaw planters are discussed in Lawrence Fay Brewster, *Summer Migrations and Resorts of South Carolina Low-Country Planters* ("Historical Papers of the Trinity College Historical Society," Ser. XXVI [Durham, N.C., 1947]), pp. 26-27.

[15] "Hesse" (Mary Motte Alston), the youngest daughter of William Alston, married William Bull Pringle. See genealogical table.

and who stated that he had been once called to see an old "wrecker" on the coast. In his cabin he saw the above mentioned portrait. After paying his patient some visits he was told that he had no money, but as he seemed to admire that picture he would give it to him for his services. On inquiry he was told that long years since, a vessel had been cast ashore and in the cabin he had found this portrait and some pieces of silver—which seemed to leave no doubt as to the fate of the long-lost Theodosia. There can be no doubt of the truthfulness of that I have written, as the letter written to my Aunt was replied to by her; but the portrait may possibly have been that of another. . . .[16]

But I must hurry back to happier days at old Fairfield where all was peace. The carriage is at the door, and the four beautiful long-tailed bays with Thomas Turner on the box. I have been sent for by my grandmother where I had been in the garden with a long cane endeavoring to bag some blue birds in the hedge. She goes to one of the other plantations, Clifton or Weehawka, to distribute the winter supply to the negroes there. We drive to the overseer's house. All work is stopped, and the bales of imported woolens and blankets are opened on the piazza, and so many yards of blue or brown or white Welsh plaids, with no admixture of cotton, are measured off to each, of all ages, from the tiny infant to those so old that they have not worked for many a long year and quite too feeble to put in their claim. The cloth and all necessary "trimmings" can be taken, if so desired, to the tailor and seamstresses at Fairfield to be cut and made according to the wish of its owner. Blankets are given by rotation to husband, wife and children. I may add that these clothes last for a much longer period than one year but are, of course, distributed annually. The summer supply is given out in the spring.

But while this is going on, I am in the barnyard among the huge stacks of rice, climbing up and rolling down those of straw from which the rice has been threshed—surrounded by a number of negro boys who enter into the sport, as only boys can. But it is time to go; and, my grandmother having listened to all complaints and given her orders as to the course to be pursued in each, and having visited the sick, etc., we return home. My grandfather has nothing to do with all these matters; all is left to one who looks closely into the wants

[16] The fate of Theodosia Burr Alston, the daughter of Aaron Burr, remains a mystery. See Wallace, *South Carolina: A Short History,* p. 370 n.

of each individual—her duties are never ending—day by day she learns all that is going on and her presence is everywhere. Kindness and gentleness was a part of her nature and evidenced in her every act—but idleness was to her the "root of all evil." All moved smoothly —there was no want, and no waste.

No one was idle that I can remember, but myself, and yet I had so much to do. Did I not have to keep a careful watch over my "traps" for birds, and keep the large cage in which I kept them well supplied till every now and then I was forced to have a general jail delivery; or look after a spotted fawn, which my father, who lived some eight miles below had sent me, much to my delight, and which I had raised—till with his huge antlers he would playfully tumble me in the dust, and each time I would attempt to rise would gently repeat the sport till I was forced to remain quietly where he placed me and await the coming of some negro to beat him off and dust my clothes. But "Billy" was devoted to me, and I to him, and meant nothing by his rough and tumble play.

This was a case where heredity was stronger than environment. The last time I saw Billy is photographed as one of the recollections of my childhood days. I went to my father's plantation (named Maryetta after his mother) to spend some time with him, and I had Billy put in a huge box, built to hold him, antlers and all. My father had him put in a vacant stall, till he became accustomed to the new surroundings. The residence was in the midst of a grove of enormous pines, and as we stood on the broad piazza together, he with his gun in hand, for he had just returned from hunting, he saw Billy coming, bounding along. My father said, "Little boy, you will never see him again, you had better let me shoot him." "Never," I replied, and the last we saw of him was as he bounded over a ten rail fence, with his antlers thrown back and his tail like a white flag raised aloft, to disappear in the dense forest beyond.

My father was a keen sportsman and I believe he took many a hunt for my runaway pet; but I know he never killed him, though doubtless he did not escape in the long run. Every evening about sunset he would take his "Joe Manton" and go to the rice-fields and shoot the ducks as they would fly over from the creeks to feed on the rice. I remember his spending a portion of one summer at Bordentown, N.J., where he killed wood-cock with Cooper the actor. This was, I think, in 1825, so I was not very old at that period. Charles

Bonapart had a lovely residence near by, and I was entranced with the beautiful pheasants kept in large wire cages in his garden, and here was the first billiard table I had ever seen. In after years I would shoot very often with my father, but I was never the shot he was, although at one time I lived in the woods and fields. Well, I will come to some of these famous hunts later on. . . .

May has come, and towards its end we leave Fairfield for Charleston. How vividly do those days come back to me at this late date. The carriage and horses are crossed over the Waccamaw and Peedee rivers to the "back landing" in Georgetown, and we are all rowed over in a six oared boat. Thomas Turner is on the box, and [the carriage is drawn] by the four bays with two out-riders on horses which matched those which were driven. . . . The days of powdered hair, and knee-breeches and stockings and large shoe buckles had passed, and instead of which the house servants of the Alston family wore dark green broadcloth coats and vests trimmed in silver braid and red facings with trousers of green plush. The large dark green and red coach [was marked] with the coat of arms on the panel of the door with the motto "Immotus"—in spite of which, however, the four blood bays moved along as rapidly as the dignity of the turnout would permit. . . .

Thomas Turner was a great favorite, and was indulged and respected. He was my grandfather's most trusted "race-rider" when he owned a number of famous horses . . . when horse-racing was confined to gentlemen, and not gamblers, and was a pastime and not a profession. There were Gallatin, Shark, Comet, Black Maria, Symmetry, and many others of which I have been told. Gallatin was bought in Virginia, a yearling, for $2,000.00, a very high price in those days. He never lost a race until his groom, just before a race, struck him on the knees—carelessly, I presume, from his having bitten at him as horses frequently do when being groomed. This put an end to my grandfather's career on the turf; he was mortified at his favourite's defeat and sold out his stud. . . . These racing stables were very expensive, and the cups and purses won did not begin to cover the cost. In the summer the various stables from Carolina would meet in Virginia, and in the winter at Charleston, Columbia, Camden, etc. . . . As a little boy I took great delight in hearing my grandfather relate of these bygone days. He was apparently somewhat austere, tall and straight, with his hair combed back from the forehead behind the ear. I do not remember ever having heard him utter an oath, and swearing was not uncommon in those days, or to have seen him in a passion; but his word was law, and his orders carried out to the letter. He had accumulated a very large fortune and took his own advice in all things, and was a man of most pronounced characteristics. . . .

Soon the Sampit river would be crossed in a flat, and after a rather monotonous drive of a few hours, the North Santee, and the causeway between it and the South Santee—which was anything but a turnpike, as the corduroy road through the swamp between the rivers would testify. To drive up the hill from the flat's landing and greet old Mrs. Williams, who kept an inn there for many years after, occupied but a short time. How often have I taken dinner or passed the night under her roof, where all was so simple, clean and comfortable. On the present occasion, if I had been older I doubtless would have seen a change in my dear grandmother's expression, for she was now on South Santee, the home of her girlhood. . . . I have often heard my grandmother . . . say that when she lived on Santee as a girl, large flocks of green paroquets could be seen, but they had disappeared before my day.

But the travelers are nearing the "32 Mile House," nearly halfway between Georgetown and Charleston. This was a noted stopping place between the North and the South, when travel was accomplished by stage coaches. Here in this out of the way place one would often meet quite a crowd of people. The road was two or three miles from the ocean in the sandy-piney woods. Good fare was generally had here; venison, wild-turkey, and duck, together with oysters and fish. The building was nothing to boast of, two houses near each other. In the space between were a number of white rabbits which were always a pleasure to me. . . .

But another day has come, and all is ready—the carriage at the door, and I climb up to take the last look at the rabbits nibbling their breakfast of cabbage leaves. A spring day on the coast of Carolina is peculiarly lovely—the yellow jasmine hangs in festoons from one tree to another, filling the atmosphere with its fragrance. The magnolia, the sweet bay and honey-suckle are all in bloom, and the dogwood spreads its green-white sail, as we move along amid the forest of tall pines. Even the little jug-blossom, along the branches, lends its delicate perfume to the sweetly laden air.

At noon we have to let the horses rest from their gentle labors, and under the shade of an enormous live oak over which had climbed a gigantic wild grape vine we take our midday repast. Over head the long grey moss is hanging amid the tender leaves of green, fit representatives of old age, and childhood beneath. . . . In the afternoon we reach the end of our journey and are rowed over the Cooper river by eight negroes who crossed to and from the city during the day, winter and summer. I so well recollect the enormous development of the muscles of the arms as they pulled at the huge oars and how massive were their chests. The old King Street Mansion is open for our reception. Servants were always left at the city and country homes, and there was no "putting to rights" in those days. Southern homes among the wealthy were always ready for occupancy, and if the owners were away, well bred servants would entertain their owners' friends with becoming politeness and respect.

This old house was built some time before the revolution of 1776 by Miles Brewton, the brother of Robert Brewton, the father of Rebecca Motte. This is the only residence in the city of Charleston, of the olden time, which has never been out of the family, and so I designate it as the Brewton-Motte-Alston-Pringle Mansion. . . .[17] It is situated on King Street, near the South Battery . . . and was built of brick and stone; all the material was brought from England, brick, stone, slate, tile, wood, etc. The lot is very large, extending from King to Legare Streets. The house fronts east on King Street. You enter through heavy iron gates and *chevaux-de-frises;* stone steps on each side lead up to a stone portico and heavy white columns. [There is] a broad stone hall [with] rooms to the right and left, and [a] broad stair way to the drawing room on [the] second story. The latter is a beautifully proportioned room, with high arched ceiling and a very handsome chandelier; among the portraits here . . . [is that] of Miles Brewton in pink silk doublet. You notice a scar on his forehead; but this wound was given as he

[17] Mr. Alston errs slightly here: Miles Brewton and Rebecca Brewton Motte were brother and sister—children of Robert Brewton. There are a number of available descriptions of the beautiful home built about 1765 for Miles Brewton. It is now generally open to the public. For description and sketches see Alice R. H. Smith and D. E. Huger Smith, *The Dwelling Houses of Charleston South Carolina* (Philadelphia and London, 1917), pp. 93 ff.

now hangs, defencelessly on the paneled wall, a British officer having thrust the portrait with his sword.

During the Revolution the King Street mansion, then owned and occupied by the widow Rebecca Motte, was taken possession of by Lord Rawdon, and Colonel Balfour and suite. Mrs. Motte refused to give up her home, but always sat at the head of her table in the large drawing-room and commanded the respect, at least, of his lordship and followers. . . . Mrs. Motte had no guard save old Allard, a West Indian negro, who faithfully slept at the door of her bedroom. I remember Allard quite distinctly, with his bald head and French pronunciation; he had all the silverware in his charge at Fairfield, and his whole occupation was to see that it was kept bright.

The British did not destroy any of the furniture of the house, but I regret to say that during the War between the States, General Hatch, of the Northern army, concluded to occupy the same house as his head-quarters. . . . By the merest accident the same old time-honoured furniture was saved by the family just as it was about being stowed snugly away in a steamer for the North. The drawing-room, as I have said, was a beautiful room with arched ceiling. Hatch knocked a hole through this, that the "beautiful stars and stripes" which the North desecrated, might float over the time honoured mansion. Well, war is a terrible thing, but it does make a vast difference as to who you fight with. . . .

As you enter the King Street house, the parlor to the left, called the South or "yellow parlor" from the colour of the damask covering of the furniture and the curtains, was the English Commander's official room. . . . The large mirrors, and beautiful marble mantle, and the white doves in fresco on the ceiling are there now as of yore. I cannot well forget them, for it was in this room that as a school boy I always slept—a little bed was put there for me and removed in the morning, and I can see the snowy doves now as they coursed around the ceiling as I lay awake. . . . In the rear is the large garden, extending to Legare Street. [Here were] the broad walks of fine shells from the West Indies, with rows of orange trees on either side, the plots of grass, the huge pear trees from which the fruit could only be secured as it fell on the green sward, the little ground doves that made their home amid the shrubbery, and the partridges that would fly across the Ashley river and build their nests in some hidden corner. A high wall of brick with wide arches protected the entire place, and I must not forget the enormous magnolias in front and the walled fruit which hung just out of reach of peach-loving children. An English gardener kept all in perfect order and supplied all the vegetables of the season. It was here that I learned my first lessons in gardening, which has ever been a passion with me. A pair of stone steps led to the garden where I, some years older, kept my numberless pets: fantailed pigeons, tumblers, pouters, etc.; rabbits, guinea pigs, squirrels, cranes, and other birds and animals. I had but little time for books with so many duties before me—indulged, petted, and spoiled as I was.

My grandfather always had a family dinner every Saturday when all of his sons and daughters and their children were expected to attend, and only a valid excuse was received for not so doing. These dinners were given in the "yellow parlor," . . . the table extended across the room, and the beautiful damask, china, glass, and silver were conspicuous. My grandmother used to send me to the attic, where the wine rooms were, to bring down the kinds of wine she wished. After having the decanters filled she would always taste, to be certain I had not made a mistake, and I would always follow her example, and so I learned, at a very early age, to discriminate between the various kinds of wine, their ages, etc.

I remember long, long years after I was at a large dinner party at my friend's lovely residence in Buncombe, North Carolina (Alexr. Robertson of Charleston, S.C.) Before we left the table he produced a bottle of very old wine and remarked that no one at the table could tell what kind it was. There was a general guessing and I said nothing, for my thoughts were far away to the days of my childhood, and the image of one so inexpressibly dear to me floated before me and I was silent. At length our host said, "Why, Motte, you have not spoken." "I know the wine," I replied. "It is '[Luna] Maderia'; it has been many years since I have tasted it, but I am not mistaken." I then told the little incident much to the amusement of the company and chagrin of some.

My grandfather imported his wine by the pipe, and as he died in his eighty-fourth year, it does not seem as if it shortened his days. The old servants have told me what a gay old time was sometimes witnessed at the King Street house. The doors were frequently locked and no one was allowed to leave the table till the "sun came peeping in at morn." You remember that Marion jumped out of a window on Tradd Street (the house is still standing) and broke his leg rather than stand the "revelry by night." This was, however, a most fortunate leap for the Americans, for he left the city before its surrender, and so saved to the cause of liberty one of the most remarkable men of the times.[18] He had the bad taste to drink only vinegar and water. . . .

When my uncle, Joseph Alston, was Governor of Carolina, large dinner parties were given at the old King Street house. He was not an ambitious man, but Aaron Burr instilled into him some of that of which he, himself, was somewhat over stocked. His death, however, soon followed the tragic end of Theodosia. In the drawing-room is the full length portrait of my grandmother Alston, en train and powdered hair. The likeness was taken in Charleston and finished in London by some eminent artist there. That of Miles Brewton, which hangs near by, is by Sir Joshua Reynolds. During the Civil War it was impossible to remove the large frames of these portraits, so they were taken out and carefully rolled and sent to me in Columbia for safe keeping, with valuable silver, old wines, etc. I will here add that, although I lost so heavily by the burning of the city, I saved all that was committed to my care; so you see there is something in luck. . . .

My aunt, Mrs. Thomas Pinckney,[19] lived for many years previous to her death next to my grandmother, her sister. I always called her "Greaty," not from her size, for she was quite diminutive, but because she was my great aunt. She always took tea with her sister and as a little fellow I would escort her home.

I remember quite distinctly seeing La Fayette in Charleston when he last visited America, in '25 or '26. Of course I was small of stature then, but I was sent to take my place under the porch of St. Michael's. A servant held my hand to protect me from the crowd. . . . The far more remarkable feature, to my eyes, was the cocked hat, or chapeau, which the distinguished French general wore; and yet after so

[18] This incident is recounted by Harriette Kershaw Lieding in *Historic Houses of South Carolina* (Philadelphia and London, 1921), p. 6.

[19] Frances Motte married, first, John Middleton and, second, Major (later Major-General) Thomas Pinckney. Smith and Smith, *Dwelling Houses of Charleston,* p. 132.

many years had passed when I looked at his portrait at General Lee's residence, Lexington, Virginia, a few years ago, I fully believe I recognized the great original, when as a child I watched the people of Charleston draw him through the streets with long yellow ropes attached to his barouche. I use the word great, simply from the fact that without the aid of the French we would never have gained our independence. But whether for weal or woe, I know not. La Fayette first set foot on American soil at North Island, South Carolina, an island next to Debordieu to the south, at the entrance of Winyah Bay. . . .

I have drifted far away from the porch of St. Michael's Church, Charleston, . . . where, as a child, I gazed at the French Marquis. . . . Saint Michael's is one of the finest specimens of church architecture in the United States. It was designed by Sir Christopher Wren and built in 1759 to '81.[20] The high backed paneled pews of red cedar, and lofty ceiling and pulpit, tell of its antiquity. The spire of 180 feet is beautifully proportioned, and can be seen many miles out at sea. Indeed, it was the objective point at which our Puritan friends aimed, when, for so many months, they shelled the old City by the Sea. The wonderfully sweet chimes of bells, . . . brought peace to many a troubled heart in the long ago, and joy to the little children on some notable occasions, such as the 4th July, and 28th June, when the old tune would tell how

On the twenty-eighth the British fleet
Appeared off Charleston harbor,
On the twenty-ninth it attacked the fort
And wounded John the barber.

This chime of bells were all removed, and taken to Columbia, South Carolina, for protection. But, alas, when the old time honored city fell, not by the fleet's attack in front but from Sherman's march in the rear, he found them near the State House, where they could not escape his trained military eye, and as he could not destroy them by fire, he had them all cracked, so as to render them worthless. These bells were sent to London and re-cast, and strange to say, at the same foundry where they had been originally cast, and are once

[20] George Williams, *St. Michael's Charleston, 1751-1951* (Columbia, 1951), pp. 129-51, discusses the building of the church, whose design is not now credited to Wren. Williams gives 1751 as the date for the start of construction and 1763 as the date of completion.

more in the belfry of old St. Michael's. But what shot and shell and hatred could not accomplish, the great earthquake which occurred on the 31st Aug., 1886, finally did, and the old edifice was greatly damaged, and cost a large sum ($50,000) to be fully restored, but the bells chime as they did of yore. . . .[21]

During the month of February there was a great deal of gaiety in Charleston—the St. Cecelia balls, and the Jockey Club ball, which latter wound up the racing season in the city. The Washington course, quite near the city, was generally the scene of great interest. Here the most noted horses of other states met those of Carolina. I remember perfectly the first race I ever witnessed. It was, I think, in the year 1825 or '6. The ladies of Charleston always turned out in full feather on these occasions, and the grandstand was filled with lovely women who took intense interest in the horses which were then owned by gentlemen of note. Of course my grandfather's family were not inconspicuous on such occasions, and the coach-and-four with out-riders brought the ladies to the race. This was my first appearance on the turf. My Aunt, Lady Nesbitt,[22] was on a visit to Charleston and brought me, a little fellow with long ringlets, to initiate me in the art of gambling in sugar-plums—all of which, of course, I won. But the race was a noted one, and though I could not then appreciate what a closely contended race was, I at least could remember the intense excitement on this occasion, the waving of handkerchiefs, and shower of bonbons I received when it was all over—much to my astonishment as I was wholly unaware of having exercised any great astuteness. This celebrated contest . . . was between Bertrand, Aratus, and Creeping Kate—three mile heats. Long heats of three and four miles were run in former years. At present, one mile heats is the fashion. . . . In my judgment the horses of over a half century ago surpassed those of the present day for the saddle and for driving. I remember my father owned a thoroughbred—Crusader. The distance from Georgetown to Charleston was, as I have said, sixty miles. This horse would . . . overcome this distance between seven A.M. and five P.M. and return a day or

[21] Sallie M. A. Black, *Chimes of Saint Michael's* (Columbia, 1901).

[22] In *The South Carolina Historical and Genealogical Magazine*, XXIV, 26, is recorded the "marriage [in 1797] of Maria, daughter of Col. William Alston of Waccamaw and Charleston by his first wife Mary Ashe to Sir John Nisbet." This name is usually spelled *Nesbit,* although here Mr. Alston spells it with two *t*'s.

two later "without turning a hair"; and my Uncle Tom, my grandfather's oldest son, would leave his plantation, Strawberry Hill, on Waccamaw, have his horse crossed over after 12 M. to Georgetown and reach Charleston in time to dress for the theater. . . .

But as usual, I have run away from the great races above mentioned. At the tap of the drum the horses were off; and a blanket could have covered the trio from start to finish, and pretty much so in the second and third heats, each horse winning one heat. The fourth heat was now to end the struggle of twelve miles. Here Bertrand showed his "bottom," or endurance, for which his stock was noted, and carried off the cup for which he so gallantly fought and which was won by hardly a neck. I have owned many thoroughbreds in my day, and would sometimes gallop on one of them, with a servant on another, from Waccamaw to attend the races in Charleston, where I was a member of the Jockey Club.[23] . . . The greatest compliment I ever had paid me as a judge of horses, was by a Kentucky horse trader, who lived in Charleston, by the name of Preston West. I met him over in Augusta with a lot of horses and I overheard him say to a fellow horse-man. "There," pointing to me, "is the only man I would ever trade horses with, without seeing them." I bought my first pair of horses from him and for long years I dealt with him in this line. . . . My grandfather left me some shares of the Washington race course, but my father, in some way, neglected to have them recorded in my name and so [they] were lost. In the same manner I lost a cotton plantation which I inherited from my mother, and when I applied to Master in Equity Gray of Charleston, he said that the titles had been so long neglected that I could not recover them. I believe the Alstons never placed any value on cotton lands. . . .

[23] [John B. Irving], *The South Carolina Jockey Club* (Charleston, 1857) has a number of references to Alstons. "William Alston, of Waccamaw, for many years had the most extensive stud of all his contemporaries in South Carolina," p. 163. See also pp. 168, 172, 179, 203. "One of Colonel Alston's favorite and most successful horses was the young stallion GALLATIN which he purchased in Richmond, Virginia, in 1802 as a three-year old from Colonel John Tayloe, after seeing him run the fastest mile that had been up to that time ever run in the United States. Colonel Alston gave $4,000 for him, and always considered him the cheapest horse he ever owned. Colonel Alston dispersed his stable in 1807 and among the principal purchasers were Richard Singleton, and J. B. Richardson . . . and General Wade Hampton." W. H. Mills, "The Thoroughbred in South Carolina," *The Proceedings of the South Carolina Historical Association,* 1936, p. 19.

The Charleston Race Course was at one period the famous duelling ground when the duello was the aesthetic mode of settling all difficulties among gentlemen. The stringent laws of the present day have pretty well put an end to this mode of wiping out insults, and the Code can now only be bought in some old bookstore. The silver-mounted, smooth bore duelling pistols have given way to the rifled barreled revolvers, and quick snap shooting on the street [has] superseded the old fashioned ten paces: "fire—one, two, three, stop"; and handshaking, if alive, and a champagne supper to cement the treaty of peace. The formality of a challenge is now out of fashion and the hip-pocket is now inserted in every man's trousers. Both methods are barbarous, but I am inclined to think that the old time method was the least so, as it gave one time to make his will and hope for an apology. . . .

I can so well remember the Nullification period—when Carolina wished to nullify the Tariff Act of 1832 or "go out of the Union." Andrew Jackson, then President, sent a United States war vessel to hold the little state in check. I remember General Robert Y. Hayne, having donned his uniform, made an impassioned address to the citizens at the arsenal. What the fuss was about I had little idea, but all was intense excitement, and when I rushed in to get my hat and join the throng, I found that my dear grandmother had pinned on it a "blue rosette" and said to me, "My son, your father is a nullifier and, of course, you are one." That settled it forever—the "blue cockade" and her dear words were worth all the Andrew Jacksons that the White House could hold. This was my first lesson in political life, and the sweet smile with which it was given will never fade from my memory.

It was time that I should begin to think more of study than play, and the task was a very difficult one. To forego my winters in the country at Fairfield with my dear grandmother was dreadful to contemplate. But I had run loose long enough, and the restraint and separation was hard to bear. So I was led like a lamb, and a pretty frisky one, to the slaughter, and placed with the Reverend Jasper Adams, President of the Charleston College, as a boarder in his family, and to attend the grammar school attached to said college.[24] I was the

[24] See J. H. Easterby, *A History of the College of Charleston* (Charleston, 1935), especially pp. 74-75, for Adams' connection with the college.

youngest boy of all the—shall I say—students, and sometimes the professors would sit me on their knees during recitations. But the boys began to tease and laugh at me, which made me kick at being petted, which culminated in my being well thrashed. This was the first time in all my life that I had been punished and I will never forget the novelty of the situation, which, with the injustice, made a profound impression on me. To cry, or evince the slightest evidence of pain, among a room full of boys, was not to be thought of, and so when I was told to hold out my hand and receive sundry severe blows with a heavy strap on each, no Spartan boy could have evinced a greater disregard of pain—to the great mortification of the teacher and approval of the class. But I had won my first fight by endurance and received the well done of my comrades. . . .

My mother's youngest brother, my uncle Dr. B. Burgh Smith, was at the time I write a student at this college; he was much attached to me and I to him. One day he got into a fight with one of the professors and I remember how excited I was, and jumping on one of the desks and shouting to him to give him something, quite a reverse of heaven. I went to see him at his home that evening to congratulate him, but was terribly disgruntled when he told me that he would probably be expelled. I begged him to make every apology, and so he was only suspended for a little while. But alas! my love for him brought me into great trouble. Feeling home-sick one evening I ran off from Mr. Adams and hied to the home of my boy-uncle, who with his brother, lived on a street not far off. I came in just as they were sitting down to a comfortable supper. I was in high spirits and they were only too glad to have me. Upon inquiry, however, they found that I had no permit to leave. I made light of it and told them that "old Jasper" would never be able to track me; and I was just beginning to enjoy my freedom when a thundering knock at the door burst the bubble of my transient happiness and ushered into my presence no less person than the old President himself, who quietly took charge of me and nearly got my boy-uncle into trouble for harboring a runaway. It seems that the son of the President, a boy of my age, had seen where I went and so spoiled my night off. Well, I was led back and sent to bed, and told to be at the President's room in the college building next day at a certain hour, which meant certain trouble for me. Well, after a good night's rest I slipped into young Adams' room and finding him in the same dress, or rather undress, as I was, we fell to and then and there settled the little difficulty between us. I managed to get him down and pummeled him to my heart's content. At breakfast I had slim rations, which was a poor preparation for what was to follow. At the appointed hour, I, to the minute, knocked at the President's room. On entering he carefully locked the doors and took from his book-case, not a volume relating to the moral delinquencies of boys roosting out at night, etc., but a regular built horse-whip, armed with which he rushed at me without warning. I was a little fellow and he was six feet; but I was as active as a young deer, and the way I jumped over chairs and under tables, totally regardless of the contents thereon, soon took the wind out of the sails of my pursuer, and the wild strokes of the whip fell in heavy blows on furniture almost as innocent as I was. Not a shadow of a touch fell on me, and I was dismissed with the admonition to do better or the dose would be repeated.

. . . I must give a pen picture of the Reverend Jasper Adams, a really good man and very intelligent, but singularly queer in appearance and in manner. He was an Episcopal minister and a native of New England (Boston, I think), was tall and straight and angular in shape and manner, wore heavy gold spectacles and had a most decided squint, and was always dressed in a full-dress suit of black. He owned, and rode almost daily a tall raw-boned horse of the same favorite color, who carried a high head and tail. The latter was "nicked" and was not overburdened with hair and moved with the regularity of a pendulum from one side to the other. The rider sat as straight as a shingle and turned his head, on which sat a tall silk hat, from side to side with almost the same freedom as did his horse's tail; and his whip, to which I have alluded, was held in his right hand, the tip nearly touching the right ear. Horse and rider were well known in Charleston. . . .

Once the President was very ill with measles and the family were ordered not to go near his room. The writer had a great curiosity to see how he looked when he was ill in bed, and really he felt full of sympathy for him, so he quietly stole into the darkened chamber and drawing aside the curtain asked him "how he was?" The effect was magical, all austerity had vanished and only words of kindness fell upon my ear and so from that time to the close of my sojourn in his house I received nought but gentleness from him.

I remember my grandmother invited him to make a visit, during the vacation, to Fairfield, and one day a large dinner-party was given. Among the guests were my father, and Captain Tom Petigru, U.S.N., a brother of James L. Petigru, the famous wit and lawyer of Charleston. Now Mr. Adams could never overcome his in-born stiffness, and the Captain, wishing to have a little fun at his expense and being a "wag," in the course of some remarks, while the large family party were assembled in the drawing-room before dinner said: "Now there is Mr. Adams, a very learned man, but with not one particle of common sense." Poor Mr. Adams sat as rigid as a poker, and the party hushed in silence. The old sea captain, having had all the fun he wanted, turned politely and said to Mr. Adams: "Why, my dear sir, I hope you did not think I would have been so rude as to address so unbecoming a remark to you? I assure you I meant little Johnny Q." The President only cleared his throat, as he tried to gulp down this timely apology.

I believe it is always best to say what part of any kind of fowl you would prefer, when asked at table, in spite of Colonel Carter of Cartersville's experience with the "one legged goose." Mr. Adams could never carve, or even help one to any dish more difficult than one of hominy. It so happened that before him was a pair of wild ducks, and after the same had been scientifically carved for him by one of the servants, he asked my father if he would be helped. I watched the proceeding, for I well knew the worthy pedagogue, though *au fait* on philosophy, did not know a leg from a wing when on a dish, and was rather slow to discover what his own legs were good for, from my personal experience in his study, with closed doors. "Have you any choice?" "None whatever," my father replied, whereupon he was helped to the two necks. You see my father was a guest there, and I at home, and so I naturally felt his "neck, or nothing" luck. But I never knew a more genial guest or host than my dear father was. His fund of anecdotes and wit was never exhausted, and he was the life of a dinner party. I once witnessed how perfectly self-possessed he was when a servant, accidently, up-set a plate of turtle soup over him at a large dinner party. He was conversing with some one and he never ceased his small talk, while the mortified servant was mopping up the steaming soup from coat and vest, and never showed to host and hostess, the slightest concern, though to sit out a long dinner and a drive of seven miles home with the odor of turtle soup about one was, at least, trying to a man's comfort and politeness.

I do not know if Mr. Adams was related to the Adams of Mass. I remember he wrote a book on "Moral Philosophy." It was a very large volume and as soon as published my grandmother bought a copy and gave it to me. I turned it over time and again and wondered what it all meant, for it was all Greek to me. But I remembered a saying of my grandfather's, "Never look a gift horse in the mouth," so I closed mine, also the leaves of my ponderous present, and laid it carefully aside for future development. . . .

My grandfather was now growing too old to take the journey to and from Fairfield, [and] then lived all the time in Charleston; . . . I would go to school in the day, but in the long winter evenings I would draw up a little chair at the feet of my dear grandmother while she would knit, and tell me of her early life, and what would I not give to have noted down all I heard. . . . But . . . little anecdotes and incidents have faded away from my memory. Her joys and her sorrows were mine, and I laughed and shed tears with one who was all in all to me. The wild life of her oldest son, and the untimely death of my Uncle Motte, her youngest, were ever present. . . .

The tragic death of my Uncle Motte was a fearful blow to his mother. He was the very joy of her heart. The Reverend John Pierpont, poet, etc., of Boston was engaged as a private tutor in my grandfather's family.[25] After living at Clifton or Fairfield in the winters and Debordieu in the summers, he took with him to Litchfield, Conn., the four boys—Thomas, Pinckney, Charles, and Motte—to prepare them for Yale College, where they were all duly entered and all in the same class. Thomas and Charles left, and only Pinckney (my father) and Motte graduated. The latter was a very bright boy and graduated in the same class with my father. He was only fourteen. . . .

The four brothers had mounted their horses and went on their way to [the] Club from the old house on Debordieu. . . . After riding a mile, Motte said, "I will overtake you, as I have to return for a moment"; and when asked why he said, "Well, I have not told my mother goodbye," and was soon out of sight and by the side of the one he loved so fondly, and telling her how dear she was to him. He little

[25] Pierpont was the grandfather of J. P. Morgan. See John K. Winkler, *Morgan the Magnificent* (New York, 1930), p. 27.

believed that he had "kissed his last goodbye." . . . At the Club an impromptu race was gotten up, and Motte volunteered to ride a very vicious horse. His brother Pinckney earnestly pleaded with him not to ride that vicious horse; but they all galloped to the ground and he [my father] alone remained, having determined not to countenance the race by his presence. After a little while, as if impelled by foreboding evil, he mounted his horse and went after them, and only in time to see his brother thrown against a pine stump, his horse having bolted. He reached him only to feel his heart give one throb and he was dead. . . . The blow was so great that the watch which he wore on his fob stopped at the same moment and so recorded the exact time of his untimely death. This watch was the one which my great grandmother Rebecca Motte wore during the revolution and was given to me. It was ever hung near my grandmother's dressing table and never wound up, but remained a silent memento of the sad event.

My grandfather and my Aunt Brewton had gone to the Virginia Springs and so when the fearful intelligence was conveyed to my grandmother she drove to the Club-house and taking her dead boy beside her with his head in her lap, she drove back to where he, in the exuberance of life and of love, had pressed on her lips his last "goodbye."

I remember after my return from college, I was driving to Magnolia Beach—the same where in the fall of 1893 a fearful storm swept the coast, and drowned poor Arthur Flagg and his whole family and guests at his house, nine in number—to see a sick friend; and as we were driving slowly over the sands I met a gentleman who stared at me, even after I had passed him, that on my return I asked my father who it could have been. He told me his name was Heriot, and that it was he who had urged his brother Motte to ride that fatal race against his own pleadings, and that ever since his mind was un-balanced.

Whilst on this subject I will mention a little incident which was somewhat singular. About this same time of the year a little girl of my uncle, Dr. Smith, died and we were taking her body to the Oaks. The Oaks was the burying ground of the Alston family for many generations. It is on the plantation so called from the number of beautiful live oaks. It was raining hard on our return and we were wrapped in our own thoughts. Now I never knew just where my Uncle Motte had been killed, this having occurred so long ago before I was born, but I was looking through the glass window of the carriage and was thinking of one whom I had, of course, never seen, and wondering if it was near that spot at which I was looking that my uncle had been killed. At that moment my father touched me and said, "Your uncle was thrown against that light-wood stump" (charred pine), pointing to where I was then looking. We had not exchanged one word on the subject and I had passed the spot hundreds of times before. Perhaps the occasion had naturally occasioned serious thoughts but even then it was singular. But I am ever getting ahead of my boyhood days.

I left off, I think, at the time I used to spend the long winters alone with my grandparents. On Sundays my grandmother always rode to church in her carriage, but in the afternoons she always walked, in order that the servants might attend if so inclined, when she and I would always be seen together in the old family pew of Saint Michael's. My grandfather at this period never left the house, save now and then to walk as far as the large stable on the premises, and look at the horses, and talk to me about them. I remember distinctly on one of these occasions his telling me, when out of ear-shot of all, that he was going to leave my father Weehawka and the negroes thereon, which was [valued at] over $225,000. "Now, my boy, say not one word of what I have told you." It seems that he had told my father that he would leave him out of his will if he contracted his second marriage. . . . And though he did marry against his father's wish, and knowing full well that the latter never said what he did not mean, it was natural that he for many long years fully believed that the threat would be carried out, if not to the letter, at least to his disadvantage. I kept the secret well, and it was only after many long years and when my grandfather was too old to change his will—which, by the way, he never would have done—did I tell my father of what property he was to inherit. He looked at me very inquiringly but of course could not blame me for keeping a secret committed to me. . . . And when the will was read, and when there was much excitement from the large amount of property in question, my father's share was just what I had told him. The relationship between father and son had not been at all strained; only my father was not consulted as to the making of said will. . . .

I would spend the months of December and April at Maryetta, Waccamaw, which were my vacations, when I would shoot at everything that came within the range of my little double-barreled gun: a beautiful one, by the way, given me by my Uncle Charles Alston—long barrels and very small bore; and you will laugh when I tell you that it was not, though of the best English make, a hammerless or even a percussion, but a flint-and-steel of the most approved pattern and latest style. In those days the wild pigeons were plentiful on Waccamaw in cold weather—now seldom or never seen; and the limbs of the cedar and wild orange trees would bend with the numberless robins, and a dozen or more [were] killed at one discharge. Now but few come. These were halcyon days. My father gave me a long-backed flea-bitten mare, of the "marsh tacky" breed; three boys could easily be accommodated at the same time and have room to spare. You can well imagine how fearfully fast the days rolled by, and how the return to school ever loomed in the near future as a purgatory with new appliances of torture artistically arranged. . . .

I learned to ride and shoot at an early period of my life. My grandmother would make a servant take me before him on one of the large bays and gallop all over the city. Of course I felt (being not much larger than a good size doll) that I was going up to the moon, but it gave me confidence knowing that strong hands held me.

I then had a pony on which I would ride to the grammar school of the Charleston College and then turn him loose and let him scamper back home at the other side of the city. Sometimes he would prefer the side-walk, to the discomfiting of pedestrians. Blue-coated policemen never paraded the streets in those days; we had [all the] states rights and city rights and charter rights that one desires. Now negroes in blue coats are the order of the day.

King Street was the shopping street of Charleston, and in the fall of the year in the long ago it would be blocked up by hundreds of wagons, each with six horses, on the collars of each were hoops, on which were fastened numberless bells which would ring incessantly. These wagons would come from the interior of South and North Carolina, laden with cotton and farm products, which when sold on the Bay would return with groceries, dry-goods and notions. This was a gala time for the waggoners, who were sometimes on the road, coming and going, for many weeks. At night they would camp out (and for mutual protection would usually keep in a long line of nearly half a mile or more) around a cheerful blaze of lightwood knots. They would while away the evenings, with old stogies, corn whiskey, and the fiddle.

Travelers had to be polite to these jolly fellows far away from home. I remember an amusing story told of a gentleman who had driven out of the City to a ball in the country. Mr. Manigault was refined and polite; and on his return home at a late hour in his gig (a two wheel vehicle similar to the present road cart only much higher) he encountered a jolly set of these fellows, who occupied the road and would not let him pass. After much persuasion they came to a compromise. He would be permitted to proceed if he would alight and dance a jig for their amusement to the music of their fiddle. Finding that this was the only method by which he could reach his home in the city, he stepped out and, taking off his cloak, displayed his ball costume, powdered hair, dress-coat, frilled shirt, knee-breeches and pumps, and danced easily and gracefully to their infinite delight, and so was allowed to pass in his gig; but not altogether liking the ludicrous figure he had cut, he quietly took from the box under the cushion of the seat, a pair of hair trigger duelling pistols, and firmly told his tormenters that if they did not in turn dance for him, he would, at least, bag two of them. And so the fiddle began to talk again, and the country boys to dance, and to swear, that in spite of his city rig, he was a very smart fellow. . . .

My quiet winters with my grandparents in the old house in Charleston will never be forgotten. When the first of April drew near, I was happy and miserable, happy to go into the country on Waccamaw where my father lived, and ride and shoot, and miserable to leave one I held so dear. I remember my grandmother saying to me as she looked at the vane, in the shape of a black fist, above the chimney of one of the out-houses: "The wind is fair and one of the vessels, the 'Martha Pyatt' or 'Little Jack' will soon be in, and then you can go to Waccamaw for your vacation." A fleet of vessels would come from the sea-ports of New England to bring the rice from the plantations on the various rivers to market in Charleston; and when the season was over would spread their white wings, like migratory birds, for their homes at the North. Steam put these vessels to flight, and the horn of the stage-coach no longer aroused the sleepy inmates of the closely packed vehicle, to a genial supper at the old thirty-two mile house, as steamboats conveyed both freight and passengers to the city [and did away with the need for stage coach as well as sailing vessel] . . . .

After a while I was removed from the grammar school and sent to that of Christopher Coates on Wentworth Street.[26] Here was in full blast the most celebrated school which Charleston ever boasted of, but one to which I never took too kindly from the first day to the last —a period of over two years. Mr. Coates was an Englishman, a trained pedagogue of credit and renown. He was a dyspeptic, and had but one eye, but that never failed to detect the slightest fault, . . . which his rattan (called by the boys the "yellow doctor") most persistently attempted to eradicate on each and every possible occasion.

This teacher most religiously and conscientiously believed that no boy, never mind how studious and perfect his recitations may have been, could be thoroughly educated unless he had been scientifically treated by the aforesaid "yellow doctor." [He believed that] his treatment was as essential in order to escape dense ignorance as vaccination to guard one from small-pox; or, I should more aptly put it, [as] venesection to cure bilious fever, for both the "yellow doctor" and lancet are now instruments of the past and only live in the recollection of those on whom they had been applied. Of course the treatment was mild or severe according to the nature of the disease.

The *modus operandi* was this: before the school was dismissed the "doctor" would visit the different rooms and as he entered would tap his own leg with the instrument, just to feel if it was keen. The boys sitting all around the room on benches, at their desks, were expected to give what numbers each had received that day. Five was the intermediate number; below it you were flogged; above it, passed. All the various arts were resorted to—stuffing atlases under jackets, a handkerchief down the rear of one's trousers; but if [these strategems were] found out, some more tender spot would be attacked by this trained and skilled masseur, who would always insert the icy cold fingers of his left hand down your collar and warm you up with the rattan he so skillfully held in his dexter claw. . . .

---

[26] Colyer Meriwether, *A History of Higher Education in South Carolina* (Washington, 1889), pp. 30-37, describes the celebrated private school conducted in Charleston, 1820-1850, by Coates, spelled *Cotes* by Meriwether.

I was awfully discouraged, at the start of this school career, and no one living knew why I cared so little about study. In the afternoons I could take my choice, either to study for the morrow, or play, and I weighed the whole thing in my mind. My cousins, the Haynes and the Pringles, had very ambitious parents [who] made their sons study all the afternoons and recite their lessons to their fathers, who were very jealous of their sons' standing at school. I felt very sorry for them when I heard them being punished, and so I concluded that as life was reported to be of short duration, there was no use to be bedeviled morning and evening. I had an over indulgent grandmother whose only words were love and tenderness, but who was most anxious that I should stand well at school; but the discipline was too rigid for one who had been educated in a different school, and so I amused myself in the afternoons and would go on South Bay in the summer and swim around the vessels and leave the latin and greek for a more convenient season—which was, I am ashamed to say, when the covered wagon, with seats at the side, which my grandfather had had built to convey his grandsons to school, was at the door and the sleek mule was urged to move off (and I may as well add as unwillingly as I did). . . . I would open my books and say to my cousins, "Come boys, I did not have much time to get into the merits of today's lessons, and you have all been well drilled; let me hear what Caesar was after when he crossed the Rubicon." . . .

I remember "Old Christy," as we called him, made a visit to my grandmother, and complained of my not being up to the mark in my studies. "Oh, dearest," I replied, "don't worry yourself about me. The fact is I can't well get on with the old fellow, and when I am strong enough I have sworn to thrash him out of his skin, for he has left on me a black and blue mark which has prevented me from going in swimming, as I don't like the boys to ask me how I came by it." I was not scolded, and all the sympathy was on my side. . . .

Well, things went on in this way for some time. Mr. Coates would be invited to spend a portion of the vacation on Waccamaw, and this was our time of reckoning. He would always bring his gun and we would have much fun out of him, placing dead birds on a tree and induce him to shoot at them and laugh at him for not killing them, rolling him over in the sand and sometimes hitting him heavily with switches. All of which he took in good part. He acquired quite a fair fortune and returned to England when too old to handle boys to his satisfaction, some of the older ones getting the better of him. He died in England, and I recollect, as some of his investments were in Georgia, and [as] I was then living there, I was asked to administer on his estate there. I remarked that I now was better fitted to do so, as he had administered on me pretty freely when a little boy.

I managed to pick up some crumbs of knowledge under his administration, however, when my father thought that this school was not the place for me, and concluded to send me to Saint Mary's College, Baltimore. This was a great blow to my dear grandmother, who could not bear the idea of my being sent to a Roman Catholic College. She could not be reconciled to it, but my father took a right view of the case. He knew that I had been spoiled and petted all my life and it was necessary that I be sent off from home. It was pretty severe, but I made no complaint, for I saw that there was one who suffered far more than I did. [There was] only love on my part, but love and religion on hers—that religion which was so simple and so pure, whose source sprung, not from a creed, but from an every day exalted life. And so with her last gift, a Bible and prayer-book, and money enough to purchase a handsome watch, I bade adieu to one whom I loved so fondly, little dreaming that it was to be forever.

We took one of the little steamers which plied between Charleston and Baltimore, the "Georgia." It was my first sea-voyage that I could remember, and I was glad to know that I was proof against sea-sickness. The night we were off Hatteras we had a fearful storm, at least I was told so, for though the little boat pitched and rolled I felt sleepy enough to go below and turn into my berth. The water began to wash over the deck and run into the cabin below and the ladies to cry aloud for fear, but all was novel to one who was then being tossed for the first time on life's uncertain and angry sea. . . . I remember my father, who had managed to climb down from the wheelhouse where he had been with the Captain, to where I was, . . . saying, "Why, you seem to be taking things very coolly when we are in great danger; you had better dress and be ready for the worst." And so I did as advised and calmly awaited the result. I say calmly, for I was not happy, and I had perfect confidence in my father, who returned to his post in the wheel-house, where he remained till we entered the Chesapeake and stopped at Norfolk. The black smoke-stack was white with encrusted salt. No boats of the present day would venture on such trips (I mean such small side wheel steamers as are now only used on the various rivers), and many were wrecked, such as the "Horne" and "Pulaski" when so many citizens of Charleston and Savannah were lost. Mr. Edward Pringle and his whole family were drowned when the former was lost. . . .

Whilst writing of wrecks, I will here relate how nobly General James Hamilton of South Carolina met his fate. He was on one of the Gulf steamers going from Galveston, Texas, to New Orleans, when the boat went down. He was on deck and had on a life preserver. It seems as if the boat had not been supplied with a sufficient number of the same, for a lady passenger appealed to him for help, and he calmly presented her with his only means of escape from death. She was saved and he was drowned. I only heard this account of General Hamilton's death lately. General Hampton related it to me and added that he knew of no more gallant death. General Hamilton was at one time governor of South Carolina, a man of ability and of a most sanguine temperament, and from this latter trait met with heavy losses. . . .

But to resume. On landing in Baltimore we went to the Exchange Hotel, the swell hostelrie of the city, but which is now the Post Office. I need not say that we lived sumptuously every day. My Aunt Maria (Lady Nesbit) was there, and if Norfolk oysters, canvass-back ducks, and champagne could lift a boy out of the depths at having been cut off so suddenly from his home in the city and sports in the country, surely our life at the Exchange would have wrought the change. But there are times when a boy does not live in the present, and after ten days I took up my abode at old Saint Mary's. . . . I had put away my juvenile clothes, and was rigged in black trousers and vest, and a fashionable dark blue broad-cloth dress coat with wrought buttons and a silk hat; I felt pretty high in my own estimation. . . . There was only one portion of my attire which choked me: I had been accustomed to wear a turned-down collar and a ribbon around it. All gentlemen in those days wore stocks which buckled on the back of the neck, and collars of the stand up variety. Now this was a stupendous undertaking for me. You know that these same stocks were made of horse-hair, covered with silk; the hair running up and down was to keep the head well up. I bought as low a one as I could find. . . . I felt as if every Tom, Dick and Harry was looking at me. I could not possibly look at myself, the center of attraction, and with difficulty at the passers by, for my eyes could only discern the chimney tops and spires of the city. No horse with an "over-check" could have felt more uncomfortable. But eels, they say, get accustomed to skinning, and so I soon learned to wear my stock comfortably, and *I* thought gracefully. At that period, 1836, Baltimore was very different from today. . . .

I remember Mr. Van Buren when President of the United States. Then a college boy, my father and self called upon him. He was most polite to us and drawing up a chair beside me said, "Well, my boy, your father tells me you are at Saint Mary's, and I hope you will come and see me when you have nothing better to do." I was a green horn in politeness then, and he was a master of the art. We visited the Senate and I was introduced to all the great men there. Calhoun, Webster and Clay were a trio which have not been reproduced; and I fear, never will, judging from and by the time of writing. . . .

When Ex-President Van Buren came South on a visit, he was given a "swell" dinner at The Peedee Club. Mr. [John H.] Tucker was president of the day. . . . He was thoroughly gentlemanly, a planter on the Waccamaw, and when I knew him had been married four times, and was known as a very ugly man, very badly pitted from small-pox, and had an enormous nose full of blue veins and a knob on the end of it. . . . After various kinds of wine had been tried and approved of, Mr. Tucker called Mr. Van Buren's attention to a very old and choice bottle, covered with the cobwebs of time, which he was about to uncork. Unfortunately the cork-screw was inserted a little too far, and on drawing the cork, the tip of the instrument pricked the blue veins on the extremity of his nose and the "claret" began to trickle down his face. A gentleman quickly tore from his beaver hat a huge pinch of black fur and stuck it on the wounded nose, which stopped the flow and allowed the President of the Club, without the slightest embarrassment, to conclude his disquisition on the merits of this same celebrated vintage. The whole scene had to be witnessed to be appreciated, and Mr. Van Buren enjoyed the hospitality greatly, and no doubt, the *black* spot formed a *bright* one to him, for some days after. . . . But the name of

Van Buren has made me drift far off from the period I was writing of. . . .

My college life was about what most youngsters experience in going through this ordeal. I had but few that I called friends, but their close friendship lasted long after our college days. . . . I had now laid aside my boy-hood days, and the surest way to become a man is to be treated like one. I had left behind me much that I loved, but also much that I most thoroughly disliked. The rigid English school-master, who believed to imbibe knowledge a pupil had to be treated hypodermically, was totally different from my views and the manner in which I had been educated. For mere book learning, I conceived, went but a short way toward the building up of a gentleman. I had a great respect for books and for learning, but the means employed to rivet the latter most securely should be gentle and not cruel, kind and not brutal. Now the priest-professors of Saint Mary's were, of course, thoroughly well educated men, and the President John J. Chamche, one of the finest, most courteous and dignified of men. During my college days nothing but the kindest feeling existed between us, and I entertained even more than admiration for him. . . .

The close confinement at St. Mary's after a while began to tell on one who had never been strong, and I wilted under the heated rooms and cold atmosphere outside. But I struggled and never wrote of my failing health. I was greatly indulged by the President and was allowed many privileges, such as sleeping late and going into the city to visit my lady friends, who, by the way, sometimes came to see me, much to the amusement of the students. But the end had to come; a cough set in, and I was fast failing. I had to take my meals alone. I became pale and had a bright crimson spot on my cheeks, which made the fellows say that I had been transformed into a girl; but the doctors ordered me to return home if I wanted to live, and so the President wrote my father of the situation and he came on at once for me. He did not come to the college but sent for me. We were both laboring under a heavy sorrow: he had lost his mother whom he was devoted to, and I my grandmother who was all in all to me. I was no longer the boy he had parted from, and we met as we had never done before; and no words passed our lips; he simply folded me in his arms. From that hour he was untiring in his devotion; he know I was suffering physically and mentally, and my precarious situation could not be concealed. . . .

On reaching Washington we went to the boat on the Potomac which was to take its passengers to Aquia Creek; but by morning the river was frozen over and the boat could not budge, so we hired a stage and went to Richmond, Virginia. . . .

We reached Richmond one night after dark and went to the Eagle Hotel. Our party was my father and self and a newly married couple. I was soon asleep, for I was ill and tired, but at about 12 o'clock I was called by my father, whose bed was opposite to mine, and advised to dress, to which I demurred, but was quietly told that the house was on fire. Half dressed, on reaching the piazza on the third floor we found the flames had almost reached the pillars, and dragging our trunks as well as we could, we found the stairway burned away; so we pulled away at our luggage to find another way down and pushing our trunks before us till we could get help. On reaching the lower floor we found firemen knocking open the doors and dragging out women and children on mattresses. The ground was covered with snow, the beautiful snow which never had any charm for me, save on the summit of some far off peak.

We soon reached another hotel, the Pocahontas, from the windows of which I watched the ill starred Eagle take its fiery flight. . . .

Of course, it was a great trial to return to my old home in Charleston. There I had passed my childhood days, and there as a boy I had learned to love the house and the trees which surrounded it, as only a boy could love a place where only peace and happiness existed, and where with lavish hands my grandparents dispensed their hospitality, and showered only joy on all who lived beneath this time-honoured roof-tree. Alas, for me! my idolized grandmother had been suddenly summoned by God to fill a higher place, if possible, in heaven.

Of course I was warmly welcomed and even the old servants among whom I had lived from infancy were profuse in their manifestations of love, and I too well remember how my heart beat in love for them. But she was not there, the one who had administered to my every want, the one who had gratified every wish, the one who had taught me what love was, and how beautiful it was to reverence all that was gentle and noble and pure, whose whole life was to pour peace into the troubled heart, and give sunshine to those who needed help, and over whom the shadow of adversity had fallen. She was not there, my childhood home was blotted out from the face of the earth, and could only live in the past, and its cherished memories.

My grandfather was near eighty and fast failing. With all the love and devotion bestowed on him in his now helpless condition by my dear Aunt Hesse, he would beg aloud for the one who was his all in life.

We did not linger long at the old home. My own health was most precarious. My father was untiring in his devotion and did all in his power to ease the burthen of my young life. He wished me to buy all I wanted, books, etc., and so we went to Waccamaw, to a plantation of his opposite Georgetown, which he had called Maryetta, after his mother. My uncle Charles lived at Bellefield adjoining, and my uncle Tom two miles below, at Strawberry Hill. Well, I came to a new home, though I was very far from a stranger, as I had been accustomed to spend my vacations whilst at school in Charleston there.

The house was in the midst of a grove of enormous pines, on many of which the yellow jessamine hung in festoons, the falling flowers dotting the russet carpet of pine straw beneath. Wide piazzas surrounded the one-storied building, and the murmuring of those ten acres of pine as the soft breeze swept through them, I can hear now as I lay awake, after some three score and ten years have swept over me; and so many, older and younger, than me have passed into the great unknown. . . .

I lived in the woods; hunting, shooting and fishing were always fascinating to me, and now I had nothing else to do. These pastimes during vacation were to be the means of re-establishing my now declining health, . . . though it took two years before I secretly whispered to myself that I was rescued from the impending fate that had hung over me for the past few years. I here will state that I never told anyone how ill I was; it could do no good and I had a half horror of doctors. I fancied I could treat my own case by eating what I deemed best, and by living in the open air and taking wholesome exercise and always in moderation. Any violent effort would have put an end to me.

When I moved to the sea-side with the family, on old Debordieu island, Waccamaw, I always suffered much for the first few weeks.

The salt air was too stimulating, and I had constant pains in the chest from the terrible colds contracted in Baltimore when at college. . . . My room in that, I might say, historic old house was the north chamber, the same where young Burr Alston died during the war of 1812. I would get out of bed long before sun-rise . . . walk rapidly to the north end of the island, on the beach, and back, some three miles, till I could by degrees make the trip in a very short time. . . . I built a canoe out of a cypress log, and with a tiny sail and awning fished during the morning in North Inlet, or among the numberless creeks between the island and the main land. . . . On my return one day, my father said to me, "I watched you as you sailed along on the rough water, with, or rather through the telescope," which was ever on the piazza. Now this same telescope was the one [with] which long years after Beauregard watched the bombardment of Fort Sumter, at Charleston in April, 1861, from my uncle Charles' residence on the East Battery. Through the same glasses were seen the perfect peace of one period, and the beginning of a war which was to change the whole aspect. . . . In the afternoons I would leave the island and gallop in the woods beyond. And so I worked myself back into health. . . .

Of course I read and studied after a fashion. Charles Dickens just then began to attract the reading world by his inimitable writings. *Master Humphrey's Clock* was published in London first in numbers, which I had mailed to me, a long way to look for an interesting novel. The story terminated in the *Old Curiosity Shop.* I also took Audubon's *Birds of America* in monthly numbers as published. I need not say with what avidity they were read, for his description of birds and their habits is as charming as the paintings are beautiful and truthful. I subscribed to the *Mirror,* edited by that most interesting writer, N. P. Willis of New York, and also to the *Albion,* an English paper published in New York. So all things considered I was not exactly growing up in profound ignorance. . . .

I remember seeing about this time a "water-spout" which was quite near in, and very beautiful. The dark clouds which over-shadowed the angry ocean seemed to bend downward with accumulated weight, and the ribbon-like stream of water connected the two. What infinitesimally small things connect those of great magnitude! . . .

With health re-established I wished to commence my long neglected studies. My father had sold Maryetta to my uncle, Colonel

Arthur P. Hayne, and had purchased True Blue, a rice plantation adjoining Weehawka, a very fine plantation which he had inherited from his father.

About fifteen miles north of True Blue there was a school kept by a German, on the seashore, I engaged a room and board there, and when the Professor would have one or two spare hours, he would come to my room, where he would smoke his pipe and I would renew my acquaintance with Virgil, Horace, and such ancients as I thought would be pleasing, by way of rounding up the education of a rice planter. I also studied Spanish with much pleasure and talked on various subjects. I had a servant to wait on me and kept a thoroughbred mare in the stable to while away some tedious hours. A deep salt-water creek was in front of the house, and there I had a goodly supply of fine oysters; and in a stall next to my mare, I kept fenced in a full supply of partridges; and thus was I finely protected from boarding-house fare. I had two companions, somewhat older than myself but who had not dipped into college life, who were fine fellows who came to learn and not play the undergraduate. Of course I kept my dogs, varied in their accomplishments; and many a night would we, with light-wood torches brightly burning . . . sally out in quest of the sly opossum, which was at this season finely flavored with the ripe persimmon. Then with a bag of this midnight game, we would sit around a live-oak fire on the shelly beach and sup on roasted oysters, freshly gathered from the deep creeks near by. . . .

It was whilst I was at this school that my grandfather Alston died in Charleston. He was very old and never rallied after my grandmother's death. . . . His remains were brought on a pilot boat from the city, and as it became known along the river a vast concourse of negroes hurried to The Oaks, and it was with great difficulty I could push my way through the dense mass of those who belonged to him and his sons, and only then to see the last spade full of earth thrown on one whom I had lived with from childhood and whom I had learned to love, honor, and respect.

These private burial grounds are very objectionable. The Oaks belonged to Governor Joseph Alston, and long before his day the Alston family were here interred; and now after more than a hundred and fifty years the place has changed hands, and, though surrounded by a brick wall, it must necessarily fall into decay.[27]

---

[27] The Oaks burial ground is now within the Brookgreen Gardens property given to South Carolina by Archer M. Huntington. The burial ground is some distance from the gardens proper and is probably seldom visited by the thousands of people who come to see the statuary and the layout of this beautiful spot. When the editor last visited the graveyard it was in good condition, and the path leading to it is plainly marked.

2

The Bachelor Planter

RICE WAS first introduced into South Carolina by Thomas Smith when Landgrave of the Province. A vessel in distress came into Charleston, the Captain of which when introduced found that he had met him (Landgrave Smith) before in Madagascar. On leaving he presented to the Landgrave a few sacks of seed rice, which he planted, or rather sowed in his garden, and distributed among his agricultural friends. It was from this source that rice became one of the staple crops of Carolina and Georgia.[1] There is a tradition that this grain was brought to the South previously; this may have been so, but, if so, it was a failure. It is rather singular that my ancestors on one side should have introduced rice into the Colonies and none of them to have become rice-planters; whereas, on the other side, so many Alstons became largely engaged in planting rice.[2]

The Cape Fear river of North Carolina, and the Waccamaw, Peedee, Santee, Combahee, Savannah, Altamaha, and Ogeechee rivers of South Carolina and Georgia, with some smaller ones, at one time produced all the rice in the United States. Now, the tidewater rice-lands on these rivers are being one by one abandoned on account of the labor being so limited and unreliable, and Louisiana and even Texas are producing very large crops of rice, under an entirely different

[1] On the introduction of rice culture see Wallace, *South Carolina: A Short History,* pp. 48-49. There are a number of records of life on South Carolina rice plantations including several by kinsmen of Mr. Alston: D. E. Huger Smith, *A Charlestonian's Recollections* (Charleston, 1950), pp. 9-56; James Harold Easterby, *The South Carolina Rice Plantation As Revealed in the Papers of Robert F. W. Allston* (Chicago, 1945); and Patience Pennington (Elizabeth Allston Pringle), *A Woman Rice Planter* (New York, 1913); Alice R. Huger Smith and Herbert Ravenel Sass, *A Plantation of the Fifties* (New York, 1941), which is beautifully illustrated with reproductions of thirty water color paintings of rice plantations by Miss Smith.

[2] Mr. Alston was descended from Landgrave Smith on his mother's side.

mode of cultivation. These last named lands are worked mostly with the plow and depend on rains and back water instead of the river for a water supply. The yield is not as large per acre, and far less reliable, as rain at a critical period is absolutely necessary, while the tide-water lands are independent of it; but the number of acres to the hand is greatly increased. There are a great many varieties of rice, some of long narrow grains and others nearly round. The golden rice is what was planted on the tidewater lands. I remember as a boy seeing the old indigo vats on the uplands of Waccamaw near the main seashores. All these had been abandoned before my day, and the plantations on the river were then in full operation. At Fairfield, I lived with my grandparents and of course such a life possessed many charms for a boy, and even at this late day I can recall the every day delights which surrounded me. Perhaps it would not be wholly uninteresting to give you some idea of what a well regulated rice plantation was in those days. . . .

Fairfield, as I knew it then, was to me a fairy land: a large lawn in front of the residence with live oaks around the drives on either side, a terrace garden of flowers in the rear extending down to a large pond, or lake, on which geese and ducks, both tame and wild, could at all times be seen from the broad piazzas. The fields and river were in the distance. Always remember that these were days before railroads and steamboats. The large rice mills for pounding rice were worked by water. The fields on which the rice was grown in summer were utilized in the winter to prepare the crop for market. The mill was erected near the river, and the fields in the rear were flooded at high water. Then the floodgates were closed, and when the tide fell in the river, the water held back in the fields was some four or five feet higher than that in the river. This then was the motive power which set the machinery of the mill's water wheel in motion; the huge stones to rotate and the heavy pestles to pound. The grain, when under the rapidly rotating stones, would not lie side-wise but on end, and so escaped being broken. The former [the stones] were [so] set as only to grind off the outer hull of the grain, called chaff; and the latter [the pestles], the inner covering, which was the coarse flour used for feeding stock. The flinty grains of rice were then carried by elevators through screens of various dimensions and, last, polished on rapidly revolving drums, covered with prepared sheep-skins. The rice for market was placed in tierces of 600 pound capacity. It took about eighteen or twenty bushels of rough rice, i.e., threshed rice, to yield one tierce of clean rice. Sail vessels would convey the tierces to market in Charleston. . . .

The rice fields of the Waccamaw were on both sides of the river. Those across the river were on different islands, so the inspection of the crop had to be made on foot, and these long walks under burning suns were, as I have said, very tiresome. Of course, all the tide rice lands are levied or banked in, so as to have them dry, or under water, as occasion demanded. The river banks had to be particularly strong to resist the strong current of the river, and the wash of the wave during storms. All rice fields (which are usually about fifteen acres in size, more or less) are banked in separately. This is done to give a rapid flow, or covering of water; or the contrary, to dry the field quickly. All the banks, or levies, must be water tight to prevent leakage in or out. When the field is under water, it is necessary that the same should be retained and when dry equally important that no water be allowed to leak in. Ditches surround each field, say fifteen feet from each bank, or four feet wide by the same in depth. Into these ditches quarter drains extend from one large ditch to the other, but only in one direction. Now, at the most convenient place, be it river, or creek, trunks are placed in order to flow the field at high tide, or to dry it at low water. These trunks, or small flood gates, are made of cypress planks, which last much longer under ground than any other wood. They are about eighteen feet long, by six feet wide and two feet deep; on each end there are uprights, slanting pieces with doors which allow the water to enter the field, or exclude it, at pleasure. As rice-planting is on its last legs now in Carolina it seems useless to write on the subject. But it is connected with the history of the past, which still clings around me, as do the sweet memories of those with whom I once lived, and who seem so far away and yet so near.

These fields, then, could be under water or so dry that the dust would arise, at pleasure. The seasons of course made some little difference—but not much to those plantations which were on the right pitch of the tide, that is, not too low down the river for salt (salt water, or even brackish, is fatal to the rice crop); and not too high up for freshets. Crops at these chosen points were never lost, from lack of water or its excess, but only from the autumn gales. And so the best land commanded from $150 to $200 per acre. These prices of course, established the value of the whole place; uplands and improvements were included in these valuations, except in extraordinary instances where expensive rice pounding mills had to be built.

These fields were plowed in winter, to turn under the stubble, and harrowed, but all the rest of the work was done by hand labor. The grain was sowed by hand in trenches twelve inches apart, the seed rice being wetted in clay and water and then dried. This process saved the covering of the sown grain, in as much as, when the water was turned on, which was called the "sprout flow" the seed-rice would remain in the trench as sown and not float out, as it would when not so prepared. This flow of water would only be allowed to remain on the field till the grain had sprouted and the little rootlets pushed into the soil. If allowed to remain one day too long, till the leaf was formed, the plant would float to the surface and be washed away. Now the field would be dried for the sun and atmosphere to cause the plant to grow till about six inches high, when the water was again put back so as to force each tiny plant to a uniform height, then dried to be hoed, and so on, wet and dry, till the fields were one waving sea of green and gold and ready for the sickle.

Rice culture on a well regulated tide water plantation, I have ever regarded as one of the most interesting agricultural pursuits. Nothing is left to chance. The field must be flowed or dried and worked according to a regular system, learned only by long experience, or instruction. The cultivation is an expensive one, and therefore mistakes are very serious. The fields are kept in garden order, no grass is allowed to grow and ripen its seed, which is so difficult to be separated from the rice when harvested together. The water grasses are killed by drying the fields, and they which flourish best when the fields are dry are exterminated by a free use of water. Rice is sown early in April and harvested towards the end of August. During this time, it is worked only by the hoe in the hands of the negro.

The Waccamaw and the Peedee rivers run parallel to each other for 25 miles, some two miles apart. All the space between is rice land, and also on the opposite side of both rivers. So from Georgetown for some twenty-five to thirty miles up the river these lands are all cleared and cultivated and in August present an unbroken view of waving fields of green with the long pendant heads of golden grain.

The rice is cut with rice-hooks and not by machinery, as the fields do not admit of reaping machines or horse power, having been under water off and on during the cultivation of the growing crop. The rice is allowed to dry on the stubble for twenty-four hours and then tied in sheaves and then in bundles, placed in large flats about thirty five feet long by fifteen feet wide and less than three feet deep, and so transported to the barn yard and stacked to be threshed by steam threshers (when the barn yards are distant the rice is threshed in the field by movable machines, but when convenient it is carried to the barn yards); and so sent to market and sold in the rough, or sent to large toll-mills where it is pounded and placed in tierces of 600 pounds average. This is the clean rice of the market. . . . Steam threshing mills cost, prior to the Civil War, about $8,000; and pounding mills some $20,000. . . . The price of rice in the rough was then from seventy-five cents to $1.00 per bushel, and clean rice from $2.75 to $5.00, per hundred pounds, but only very choice "head rice" brought the last named price. . . .

Fairfield was a model plantation. Besides the hands, necessary to make the crops, there were mechanics of all kinds: carpenters, blacksmiths, coopers, tanners, shoemakers, tailors, bricklayers, etc., etc. Men and women were employed to raise large numbers of turkeys, chickens, ducks, geese, etc. Large droves of cattle were fed on the rice-straw in the winter and turned out on the salt marshes in the summer. All the plantations extended from the river to the sea. The hogs were fed on the coarse rice-flour, and more than enough bacon was cured to supply the family and plantation. Besides, the negroes had hogs and cows of their own and poultry enough to sell.

Not very large corn crops were raised, as the up-lands were rather sandy, but enormous quantities of sweet potatoes were grown, and I have known 700 bushels gathered from one acre. This, of course, was far above the average, and this heavy yield was grown in a field of some fifteen acres of rice land. This large yield was at Brookgreen, the residence of Colonel J. J. Ward.[3] It took the prize at the agricultural society and was gathered and measured in the presence of witnesses. I only state this to show how very dry these swamp lands could be made by ditching and draining. The potatoes grown on the sea board of Carolina were much finer than those in the interior. A

[3] Susan Lowndes Allston, *Brookgreen, Waccamaw, in the South Carolina Low Country* (Charleston, 1935), pp. 23-27, identifies Ward and quotes in full a letter from him to R. F. W. Allston, written in 1843, describing Ward's cultivation of big-grain rice at Brookgreen.

sandy soil well fertilized suits them best. The best varieties were the "sugar yam," which, when baked in a large brick oven which was generally adjoining the capacious kitchen fire place, would be candied, very sweet. The proper way was to bake, say a bushel, and rebake as needed. The large Spanish potato was held in high esteem—they had a creamy color and were very large and corrugated—and the red skin, which came in in July, were of a bright red exterior and very white and dry. No one who has never eaten these varieties grown on Waccamaw, knows anything about what a potato is, and no one who has not lived there has any conception of what an abundant country this was. All that the river and sea afford was here; fresh and salt water fish could be caught, and only three miles apart. (As I have said, the river runs parallel to the ocean.) I know of no other country so favourably situated. The winter climate on the plantation was unexceptionable, perfectly healthful and delightful, whilst that in summer, on the island, only three miles away, was equally so. Health, abundance, and contentment reigned.

The negroes were a most contented people. I suppose they out numbered the whites nearly one hundred to ten, and yet a safer country could not be found. Crime was nearly unknown; petty thefts are all I can remember, save in some very rare instances. They were well cared for, bountifully clothed and fed, and housed in frame buildings with ample brick chimneys and open fire places to receive all the wood that they possibly could consume—oak and hickory, and the resinous pine, which kindled in a moment. Their winter clothing, blankets, and Scotch caps were all imported direct from England—white and blue Welsh plaids—all wool, which cost from eighty cents to one dollar per yard. No cotton material [was used] save for summer wear.

Negroes on these rice plantations worked by the task. For every kind of work there was a set task, and so, according to ability, there were full-task, half-, and quarter-task hands. When two tasks were accomplished in one day by any hand, he was not expected to work the next, and these tasks were *never* increased. The said hand would usually go to the sea shore and lay in a supply of fish and clams. Large numbers of mullet were caught at night in cast nets, and sacks full brought home. The mullet in autumn is a fine fish and the roes exceptionally so. Before side-wheel steamers were invented, large schools of these fish were taken in enormous seines. I have been told of a hundred pounds at one haul.

During the rice harvest there could be no task. From early morn, till late in the night—when torch lights were burned in the barn yard to enable the hands to see how to put the newly cut sheaves into racks—the work went on. From the time the harvest began, about the end of August, till it was over—say from five to seven weeks, Sunday excepted—there was continual work, from sun rise till late in the evening, and strange to say, it was a period most enjoyed by the negroes. With drum and fife, they marched and counter-marched, till the harvest was over, and then there was hardly a corporal's guard fit for duty for some days after.

Large rafts of boards, shingles made of cypress, hoop poles, and barrel staves would be brought from the uncleaned lands higher up the river by white men for sale to the planters. There was a house to accommodate these people at Fairfield with dining room and sleeping apartments furnished, and meals provided during their stay, of course free of all cost. A large amount of all such material was consumed on a large plantation. At Fairfield there were at least fifty carpenters to build and keep in repair all the houses, trunks for the rice-fields, etc., etc., on this and my grandfather's other plantations. These mechanics usually brought up their sons to their trade.

My grandfather owned a number of plantations, many of which had been given away to his sons. At the time I write of, there were besides Fairfield, Clifton and Weehawka; and of negroes grown, 800 to 1000.[4] The care of so many was far more arduous than you would imagine. The hospital for the sick [was] provided with careful nurses and physicians, employed either by the year or for individual cases. Then there were houses where the children were cared for during the day when their mothers were at work. All of these departments were supervised by the master or mistress, to see that the sick were carefully nursed, and the children not neglected as to food, etc.

On all well regulated plantations ministers instructed the young in their catechism, and usually a half day was given for attendance of adults on an evening service at the plantation church, or meeting-house. At a later period the church at Hagley erected by Plowden

[4] Bull, *All Saint's Parish,* p. 15, says the census of 1790 showed 877 Negroes owned by Alstons on Waccamaw Neck.

Weston for his negroes was of brick with steeple and handsome clock.[5] He was a very humane man, educated at Cambridge, England, and married to an English lady who devoted herself to the negroes on the various plantations owned by them.[6] The Reverend Alexander Glennie, an English clergyman, was the rector of All Saints Parish, for over thirty years. He was the most devout and painstaking man I ever knew. He, or one of his assistants, would preach on the various plantations, and was beloved and respected by all who knew him, both white and black;[7] but strange to say, that after the Civil War no negroes listened to his preaching, but would shout and sing after their own fashion, and surround themselves with their old African superstitions. Some will say that this was the effect of slavery; and others, a natural defect of the negro race to ignore truth, but time alone will prove whether freedom will elevate and improve their condition.

The negro's intellect is brighter at about the age of twelve. I have often noticed how wonderfully intelligent they were at this early age—quite, if not more so than whites of the same age and surroundings; but as they advanced in life, even under school advantages they did not seem to advance in intellect. Of course there were many

5 *Ibid.*, p. 21.

6 For a delightful sketch of Plowden Weston, see James Henry Rice, Jr., *The Aftermath of Glory* (Charleston, 1934), pp. 105-10. In a subsequent reference to Mrs. Weston, J. M. A. states that she was the daughter of Sir Edward Esdell. Compare Rev. William Wyndham Malet, *An Errand to the South in the Summer of 1862* (London, 1863). The preface explains the "errand": "An English lady, married to an influential planter in South Carolina, had been bereaved of three of her nearest and dearest relatives in England; but as no letter could reach her, it was determined that one of her family should convey to her the sad tidings." The lady is not identified by name but strong internal evidence points to Mrs. Weston. The book is a very interesting picture of the refugee life of the families of Low Country planters. It is strongly pro Southern. The only copy of the book known to the editor is in the possession of Mrs. Kirkman Finlay of Columbia, S.C.

7 Bull, *All Saint's Parish,* pp. 21 ff., outlines the career of this saintly Englishman. "Recollections of a Visit to the Waccamaw," *Living Age,* LIV (1857), 292-96, describes services for the Negro slaves as conducted by Mr. Glennie in 1843 on the plantations of John H. Tucker, Francis Weston (Plowden Weston's father), and Thomas Pinckney Alston (J. M. A.'s father). "On two occasions having detected some gross misconduct among [the Negro] communicants of the church, Col. A. informed them of his intention to report their sins to the rector. In each case he received a petition to adjudicate the matter privately, the culprits professing a readiness to receive any punishment he thought just, provided he would not 'tell the Parson.' But this he refused to grant, and sentenced them to the ecclesiastical censure they so much dreaded. Those who know the meek and gentle temper of the pastor, will be surprised to learn, that his reproofs possess so much of the thunder of the Vatican." *Ibid.,* pp. 295-96.

exceptions. I simply write of the masses and not of individuals. Slavery furnished the most reliable labor, but the responsibilities were very burthensome. The North did not begin to understand this, nor did its people wish to know. There were cruel masters, just as there are cruel fathers, and hardhearted overseers in the mills and factories North and East, and the comforts of well treated negroes far surpassed those of the best regulated factories. The difference lay between the words "slave" and "hireling"; and the time will come when saintly people of New England will boast of the philanthrophy of their ancestors at having brought the negro from Africa to be civilized and Christianized to the extent of their capacity by the people of the South. . . .

I remember having been told that my grandfather, having purchased some wild Africans from a slave ship which had landed in Charleston, brought them to his residence in the City before sending them to his rice plantations on Waccamaw. One day when they were sitting on their haunches around a huge pot of soup which was boiling in the open air, for their mid-day repast, my Uncle Tom, then a mischievous little boy, threw a few drops of the liquid repast on the naked person of one of these untamed creatures of the dark continent. As quick as thought, he seized the child and would have thrown him head foremost into the boiling cauldron, but for the intervention of one of the dusky guards who saved the child from a horrible death, and, I may add, cheated the wild African, of a repast better suited to his refined taste. I merely give this little incident to show the material the South had to work upon. . . .

They are a great improvement on their ancestors, judging from specimens which were brought into Charleston about 1856 aboard a slaver, which had been captured by a U.S. sloop of war, before she reached Cuba. These poor creatures were of the very lowest type of humanity, if indeed it is fair to so designate them—for only the animal nature rose superior to their miserable, emaciated condition. When one gazed in pity and in horror on these poor creatures it was impossible not to feel, even as dreadful as the slave-trade was in former years, how immeasurably superior in every respect today is the negro of the Southern States to what those of Africa are at this period. Doubtless they endured untold hardships in a great many instances but the transformation of the naked savage from Africa to the civilized, intelligent, polite and well attired gentleman and lady of color is certainly very marvelous to behold; and yet this is what slavery has accomplished. . . .

The constitution of the imported African was generally wonderfully good and he lived generally to a great age, and strange to say they were more honest than those born in the United States and were selected to fill places of trust. . . .

The summer which followed my grandfather's death my father went to Virginia for the restoration of the health of my step-mother, and I laid aside my books to attend to his now large planting interest. I lived at old Debordieu. My maternal grandmother and my Aunt Mary, my mother's sister, lived with me, and I then took my first lessons in rice-planting, which I never relinquished as a profession till I had accumulated a very comfortable fortune of about $130,000 some two or three years before the civil war.

I obtained from my father some 600 acres of land at the junction of the Waccamaw and Bull Creek, which latter is really the main stream of the Great Peedee, the same being a portion of some 10,000 acres of land belonging to my grandfather's undivided estate. . . .

The old people who lived in these parts used to tell me that when my grandfather, Colonel William Alston of Clifton, was a young man he would come to this wild region to hunt, and some say to frolic, but as to what kind of frolicking, I could never discover. I presume he put up at "Uncle Billy's" on the bank of the rapid flowing Bull-Creek river. Who Uncle Billy exactly was, I cannot with accuracy define. All that I know of this myth is that he kept a country store and that he would go to Charleston now and then, I presume to lay in a stock of goods, for the "blue home-spun" men, and the "chicken-bonnet" ladies who lived in the vicinity. On one occasion whilst in Charleston, my grandfather, when driving up King Street discovered Uncle Billy sitting under an awning with his coat off, smoking his pipe, and when he again met him he read him a lecture on the impropriety of sitting in Charleston's most fashionable thorough-fare with his coat off. His reply was that the little Jew fellow had politely invited him to do so and he did not think it any harm to have a chat with the owner of the shop. My grandfather remonstrated, and told him that when he came to the City he must not bring Bull Creek ways with him. I remember telling my father this little anecdote, and he asked me where I had picked it up and laughingly said, "I would not, if I were you, tell these stories." So I judged that Uncle Billy was not a myth but a relation, who had failed after the Revolution to get into the swim of fashionable society, or did not have the where-with-all to plant indigo or rice, contented himself to the life of a back-woods-man in Horry district. How singular, that after so many long years, I should have selected the same neighborhood, as the place of my first business venture and should have been so eminently successful in converting this almost impenetrable swamp into one of the most remunerative rice-plantations. . . .

The swamp land, which I concluded to reclaim, formed a peninsula between the two rivers, some half a mile wide. It had been granted to John Allston in 1735 and had never been touched by the axe. The growth consisted of enormous cypress, gum, ash, etc., matted together with huge grape vines, and cane from fifteen to twenty feet high; and here I lived for fourteen years. Of course, I need not say there was no society, for the Waccamaw cut me off from all the valuable plantations below, and the Peedee, or Bull Creek, from the settlement on Sandy Island where the Belins, the Petigrus, the Heriots, and LaBruces lived and also the Vaux and others.

I worried my father till I succeeded in having a division of these 10,000 acres between my two uncles and himself; and then [came] the misery of the uncertainty as to his drawing that portion which I had so desired to own. One day the three brothers met in Georgetown. My cousin, John Ashe Alston, to whom I was deeply attached, proposed to have the land divided then and there, so he tore off three scraps of paper and wrote on each the tract thereby designated, pulled off his silk hat and handed it first to his father, my uncle William, he being the senior brother, then to my Father, who drew the tract I so desired. My Uncle William said, "Pinckney, I want that which you have drawn." "Well," was his generous reply, "pay me $500 and your drawn lot and you can have it." It was refused, and not till then was he told that ten times that could not buy it now, for I had set my heart on having it. I confess I was vexed at the risk I had run. This property was valued by my father—the 500 acres I wished—at $5,000, for which he gave me credit as so much of what he intended to leave me. I lost no time in having the title drawn, and when it was mine I would go up the river in a boat, some twenty miles, and walk over the upland portion of my first possession, and speculate how I would feel when I moved into this almost unexplored wilderness of trees.

I said I had no neighbors; yes, I had one who introduced himself to me on one of my solitary visits to this future home. I was seated on a log taking my lunch, which I had in a basket beside me, when an individual stood before me, whose appearance was as unexpected as it was unique. He was of average height, but powerfully made, broad shoulders and arms of unusual length; his face was not bad, as far as features were concerned, but his expression was simply vicious, the under lip slightly protruding; and the partial stoop, as he stood before me, reminded one of some wild beast. The homespun dress and his jaws tied up in a red cotton handkerchief did not add any to the picturesqueness of this *outré* figure. "Morning, Colonel." "How are you, Captain?" For the pirate Mansfield of the Caribbean Sea, alias W. O. Clarke of Horry district, South Carolina, needed no introduction; his reputation rendered cards superfluous. The swamps were well filled with his cattle, as fat and sleek as they could well be, on the dense cane brakes, etc.; and he had stumbled on this youth who had come to defraud him of his living, I presume, was what was uppermost in his mind.

Of course, I invited him to share the contents of Basse's pale ale and poured out a horn full of the same. I say a "horn," for I had a drinking cup made of a large cow's horn lined with metal. This pleased him greatly—not the ale, but the novel cup, which he turned over and admired extravagantly, so much so that I asked him to keep it, and drink my health in the same. It was rather cruel in me. He demurred, at first, but the present rather astonished him, and his manner changed for the better; and when he left I was minus a drinking horn and he somewhat shorn of his innate hatred to an Alston. He had given the family a vast deal of trouble by his squatter-sovereignty views of possession, and so claimed a large portion of these wild lands, even though we had the original grants from King George when Carolina was a province. . . . Henry D. Lesesne, afterwards Chancellor, deserved great praise for clearing up the titles, and Clarke now held only 13 acres, by possession, in the midst of this large area. Line trees were dug up and carried off, and every device used to cheat and annoy. He always had some case in Court and was remarkably well versed in all the cunning dodges of the law; and Judge M—— told me a worse man never lived, and that nothing would induce him to live near him, and always wound up by saying, "W. O. Clarke will kill you". . . . Well, we lived near each other, hunted deer together, had some unpleasantness, but I lived to see him outlawed and driven from the thirteen acres into the everglades of Florida.

I confess that once I did feel rather queer. I had built a shanty on the bank of the river, in which I lived. It was over a mile from the settlement where my negroes and overseer lived and I was alone except [for] a little boy who belonged to me and who was my factotum, and who slept in the room next to me. One night, just before I had retired I heard a rap at the door and in walked Clarke armed, as he ever was. What he came for, I could never find out, he remained about one hour and then left without making the object of his visit known. After some years he was hard pushed for money so he ran a sloop up the river and stole two negro men from a widow who lived some miles above me, sailed to Savannah and there disposed of them and fled to Florida. I remember I had to send to his wife bacon and meal to "keep the wolf from her door."

In this shanty by the river, I lived till I was married, and a very rough life I had. But at the time of my meeting, for the first time with my future neighbor, Clarke, when he "admired out of me" my Scotch drinking-horn, this shanty had not then been built. I merely relate anecdotes of the man, as they were re-called to my mind by relating my introduction to him, when taking my quiet lunch and feeling I was a monarch of all I surveyed, but the only brute just then visible came in the shape of this newly discovered neighbor. Still, strange to say, we used to hunt together.

I will here relate what I consider a most remarkable evidence of a dog's gratitude. I never left the humble shelter that I called home without my Westly Richards double barrelled gun, and when I mounted my little black Indian pony, "Nick of the Woods," a favourite hound was allowed to follow. Thus I often picked up a deer when I was attending to business. On the present occasion I rode from the swamp into the piney woods beyond and I soon recognized Clarke, gun in hand, standing motionless. On riding up to him he raised his hand to enjoin silence and I then heard his dogs in full cry. To hide "Nick" *in* the woods was the work of a moment. When I saw a fine deer heading directly for us, without moving Clarke said, in an undertone, "Shoot." "No, it is your deer." He then fired and missed, when before he could discharge his second barrel I killed the deer. Seeing the animal struggling on the ground he fired his last barrel, which was unsportsmanlike and wholly useless.

Just then another deer came bounding up the long piney slope. There was but one barrel left, and that was mine, and so the second deer fell close by the first; but before we could secure him, he jumped up and made for the river, which was not far off. In a moment Clarke was mounted and by the time I could untie my pony and join in the chase I found that the wounded deer had leaped down the steep bank into the river and my dog after him. I saw a horse, a gun and a *coat* on the bank, and noticed the head of a man in the water. Of course I thought he had jumped in to secure the deer, and so expressed myself. "No," was his reply, "the deer has sunk and when I rode up I found your dog in endeavoring to secure him became entangled in a vine and so was drawn under the swiftly running water, and I could not stand by and see your d——d beast drown." They both came out and shook themselves, and of course, I thanked Clarke as warmly as I could; but to my great astonishment, my thanks fell far short of my dog's gratitude. He bounded up on the one who had saved him, licked his hand and gave every demonstration, far more emphatic than words could have conveyed, to this stranger, whom he had never seen before.

We rode back, picked up the first deer and concluded to continue the hunt, which we did for the rest of the day. I was invited by Clarke to break bread with him, which I did. I then met his wife, quite a handsome woman, with a bright eye and clear white and red complexion, which was singular, living in such an unhealthy region. Also, his sons, men taller than their father, and being trained by him. I know I was an object of great curiosity, for very few ever had any intercourse with the Clarkes, even in this sparsely settled country. I must not forget to say that my fine dog, which had been reared by me, could never be induced to leave the stranger who had rescued him from drowning and to whom I gave him as a memento of his unselfish act. Though only a mile and a quarter away he never returned to even visit his former home. I consider this a wonderful case of gratitude. W. O. Clarke was always my enemy, for I had fenced off his cattle from their rich feeding grounds, and he was forced to sell them.

I was informed one day that his wife had traded with my negroes, which offense, by the laws of the State, was punishable by whipping at the "Carts-tail" on the public square of the district Court-house. He came to me in great trouble about it, little knowing that nothing could have induced me to have any woman submitted to such an indignity, and I told him to make himself quite easy on that score. From that hour he gave me no trouble at all, and when we accidentally met, formal salutations only, were exchanged. His strapping, massive shoulders and his swinging gait told of his sea-faring life, and those who knew him well said that his body was scarred all over. From the coasts of Florida he found his way to the secluded spot which I have described, that neck of wild sand between the Waccamaw and Peedee, most assuredly a safe retreat. It was discovered that his real name was Mansfield, a New Englander by birth and sailor by profession which ended in joining some piratical craft on Southern Seas. An acquaintance of mine told me that long before the war he was traveling on horseback in Florida, and when at Tampa he wished to have his saddle repaired, he inquired where it could be done. In the little shop, where he was directed, he saw a man, who wore large goggles, whom he at once recognized as Clarke. There was $1,000 reward offered for him, and so, to make assurance doubly sure, he told his servant who traveled with him to go for the saddle and to tell him who he thought the saddler was—but the shop was closed and the bird had flown. Of course the visitor was recognized. So here ends a long story, told chiefly to illustrate the gratitude of a dog.

Now I must go back to where you found me at lunch, some two years before I had built my little shanty beside the river. I only came up now and then to quietly study over my plan when I should be able to purchase some 80 or 100 negroes to clean up my new possession. I moved up from my father's plantation an old African, Scipio by name, and his young wife. Scipio, true to his name, had been to the "manor born" and passed his early years in Africa. He spoke pure Gullah; few could understand his interesting dialect. Sip was delighted with the change and his bride (who was his third, fourth, or fifth wife and quite young) had nothing to do but wait on him, and he had, in turn, only to make himself comfortable. I called him my "watchman," but this estate had not been watched since Adam's day and earlier. And when I would run up from True Blue to see how he was getting on and ask him how things were, he would grin and say "berry well" (very well). I had a shanty built for him and his bride, and would send them their provisions and the only wonder was, why my trusted watchman did not sleep himself to death. . . .

[On one occasion] our guest [Mrs. Plowden Weston] was deeply interested in the dialect of Scipio, of which she could not understand one word, and so, to amuse her, by arousing his displeasure, I said to him, "Sip, don't you want to go and live at Hagley, next to Weehawka, where this lady lives?" "Don't bodder me Mossa, enty you know I bin libbin in dese woods fo' erry udder nigger mek track yer—go way and don't bodder me, or I run way fo' tru—yerry wat I say"—and to make his words more emphatic, he would draw in the air between his teeth and make that peculiar and by no means agreeable sound so associated with the negro race. . . .

Scipio, with many others, was bought by my grandfather from a New England slave-ship which came into Charleston to dispose of her cargo. He was never resold, but like most of his [my grandfather's] large number of negroes, lived and died in the same family. I can't say that I owned the old man; I simply moved him from my father's place to mine. I have shown the life he led, and now I will only add that he lived to see most of these rice swamps in cultivation; he lived to see a large twelve room dwelling built; he lived to see a steam mill in operation, he lived to see steamboats and vessels being laden with rice; he lived to see a church built for the negroes, where Episcopal ministers preached to them, and once the Bishop of South Carolina, Davis. And yet during these long years, I do not believe he was ever called upon to do one day's work; the poor old fellow escaped the freedom of old age neglected.

About this time my father bought 1,000 acres of land in Habersham County, Georgia, and built a handsome residence in the midst thereof. . . . He concluded to reside there, and I controlled his planting interest in Carolina: True Blue and Weehawka, some 600 acres of rice land. Of course, he had an overseer whose pay was $1,000 per annum. In the winter months I lived at True Blue; my grandmother Smith and my Aunt Mary, also resided there. I built a comfortable cottage at the Southern point of Pawley's Island, and there in the summer months I lived alone. I bought some eighty negroes and commenced active operations at Woodbourne, the name I had given to my plantation, and now my hard work began. After an early breakfast on the island, I would, behind a pair of fine travelers, soon reach True Blue and Weehawka, cross the river in a small canoe and walk over the crop of rice, some 600 acres, which on a steaming hot day in July, August and September, was fairly exhausting. There were on my father's places some 400 negroes, more or less; on Woodbourne from 100 to 150 as the years rolled by. Now, to daily superintend all this business was no trifling task. Of course, I did not visit Woodbourne, which was some sixteen miles higher up the river, on the same day. They who believe a planter's life was an easy one were vastly in error.

Before looking over the crop, the sick had to be visited in their own homes and the physician sent for where necessary. All minor cases were treated by the owner, who often became quite expert in the diagnosis of diseases. Nurses who had been carefully trained faithfully carried out the instructions of the physician or owner. Whilst the mothers were in the field, the children were under the care of nurses who cared for them in a large building built for the purpose, and which was daily inspected by the owner of well regulated rice plantations in Carolina. All these matters consumed time and patience. Of course physicians daily attended those who were ill. . . . Plantations often twenty miles apart, under a burning summer sun and in an unhealthy climate, often changed the physician into the patient. . . .

The plantations on the Waccamaw extended from the river to the ocean on the east, some two to four miles across that neck of land. Thus were they more favourably situated than other rice regions. And so on the east bank of the Waccamaw river were the residences and settlements of the planters, and where they resided in the winter months; their summer homes being either on the deep salt water creeks, or beyond on one of the islands which fringe the southern coast. These islands are perfectly salubrious, separated from the mainland by the deep creeks just alluded to, and washed by the Atlantic. Some of them have no trees, only sand-hills covered with a coarse kind of tall grass. Others are densely wooded, chiefly with the live-oak, magnolia, wild-orange, etc. The fishing here was very fine, both out at sea and in the deep creeks, the cavalli, sheephead, bass, sailor's choice, whiting, black fish, and numberless others. The green turtle and diamond back terrapin, the stone crab—the finest of all crabs, which are only taken by looking for their holes, which are found at low water in the banks on the sides of the creeks. Into these holes the crab retires when the tide is low and he is captured by inserting, *cautiously,* your hand and arm nearly to the shoulder and covering the crustaceous animal with your hand before he has time to raise his enormous claws and cause an exclamation nearly as incisive as the bite from his gigantic pincers. The flavour of these crabs is far superior to the common "sea-crab," and he is a dainty feeder, while the other is not.

The salt marshes between the main land and these islands are from a half mile to two miles wide. At Debordieu it was over two miles. Deep creeks wind through them where wild duck, curlews, sea-snipe, and other birds abound. Indeed Waccamaw abounded in all kinds of game, deer, wild turkey, duck of every variety, partridge, woodcock, snipe and fish of almost every variety, both fresh water and salt. The shad caught in the Waccamaw are the largest and finest in the United States and are usually sent to the New York market. In the salt creeks are found, in great abundance, the finest oysters, also clams and shrimp, etc. It cost little or nothing to live here; all one had to do was to send and get what he wanted from the woods, fields, and waters. But I dwell too long on these things.

I built, as I have said, a cottage on Pawley's Island opposite True Blue and Weehawka, and now had my hands full of work, my father's rice interests to superintend, and 450 acres of heavy rice swamp to be cleared—a very heavy and expensive undertaking. These lands had to be levied, or banked in, to keep out the tide water. Then the cane [was] cut down; and on this, all the small under growth and brush; then the timber, large and small, cut down within two feet of the ground—all the limbs cut off and cut up into short lengths, and the tree "lopped up" into logs of eight or ten feet. The very large timber was deeply girdled so as to effectually kill it. This deep mass of vegetable matter was allowed to dry for months, and then on a suitable day it was fired. A good burn was a good thing. When the fires were out all the logs left on the ground were lifted and piled horizontally together as closely as possible and again fired and pushed up with handspikes till all were consumed.

All this area of land, which I have said was a peninsula between two rivers, was divided lengthwise by a bank with deep ditch on each side, some fifteen feet from said bank; while from this center bank others were built at right angles so that one set of fields, of ten to fifteen acres, drained into one river and the opposite set into the other river, each field having its own "trunks" for flooding or drying the field. These alluvial lands were very fertile, producing enormous trees, one of which I measured, and found it twenty-two feet in circumference. I was induced to measure it when I killed a deer which fell beside it and then noticed its size. It took some years and a great amount of labor to put all this land in cultivation, but the rice which grew thereon was the finest I have ever seen, and the planters from below would frequently visit Woodbourne and admire the same. I had about three and a half miles of river bank to keep up after the great labor of construction, to say nothing of the number of miles of inside banks and ditches. This "raw" ditching was very laborious; twenty feet long, four feet wide, and four feet deep was the task of a man. Sometimes he finished his task by 12 o'clock and would go home or go fishing; but then a fair surface was not an indication of an easy task, for often an old cypress tree buried lengthwise with the ditch, where it had lain for long numbers of years—and as solid as when it fell—would take him many days to finish the same task which he had so soon completed the day previous. Thus it was that each man took the same task each day by lot. . . . This, then, was the routine of my daily life; and when I reached, about sun set, my "Cottage by the Sea," I was glad to sit on the little porch or piazza where, through a vista formed by the overhanging oaks, the old ocean looked like a lake afar off, when in reality it was only some 150 yards away.

I often look back to those days—how quietly and peacefully they were passed, and what a sweet rest Sunday ever brought me. Sometimes service was held in the parish Church of All Saints on the river, and now and then in some unoccupied dwelling on the main sea-shore, which was nearer to most of the congregation. Here we would meet in an informal manner and listen to the prayers, which are ever beautiful, of the Episcopal Church and a sermon by that most holy man of God, the Reverend Alexander Glennie, than whom He never made a purer or a better. [He was] an Englishman by birth and a graduate of Oxford who came to Carolina as a private tutor of Plowden Weston and afterwards became rector of All Saints' Parish, Georgetown District, where he had three Churches in which he or his assistants officiated, besides Churches on the plantations where service was held for the negroes during the week. Here for over thirty years he preached the word of God to white and black, master and servant, equal in the sight of God, and so equally under his care. He lived to see the negroes made free and his flock scattered. Then did he write to his two brothers in England to know if a parish could be found for him there, as thirty odd years of his life had been measurably lost in Carolina, the negroes preferring to listen to those of their own colour, who had been reared among them and were as ignorant as themselves. He subsequently became rector of the Episcopal Church in Georgetown, South Carolina, and died at an advanced age, beloved and respected by all who knew him, and doubtless is reaping the reward for the great good he did whilst on earth. Sunday was really a day of rest and reading. I so well remember having carefully studied Burket's *Notes on the New Testament*. . . .

In the "well" under the seat of my vehicle, I would keep some books locked up, which were my companions on my long rides. . . . On Fridays all the neighbors, planters and doctors—we had no lawyers, no, not one—met at [a] club at Midway, where we had a Clubhouse, large dining room, billiard and ten pin alley. Midway was a seashore place belonging to my father and where his father and grandfather had planted indigo before the introduction of rice on the river. . . . Here was, in the long ago, the training course of some of the finest racers in Carolina, and here were to be seen the old indigo vats. We all met at 11 o'clock A.M., returned home after sun set. The Club was the old "Hot and Hot Fish Club," of Waccamaw, and lots of fun and pleasant hours were there spent. We presided by turns, and each member brought his own dish or dishes, wines, etc., and so when a full attendance was present a very full table, of course, followed. Each member brought his servant; and when all the good things had been discussed, interwoven with some politics and lots of rice talk, and the table cleared of all save the bottles of old wine, the thrice told anecdotes and songs would enliven the scene till night began to throw her kind mantle over the happy members of the Hot and Hot Fish Club. Alas, all are cold now in their graves. . . .

Some of us had to cross deep fords when the tide was in, when to the right or left was bad for man and beast, water up to the top of the seats of our carriages and so in close proximity with those of our trousers, just failing to run across our horses' backs—close driving for men who had just taken enough to keep the cold out of the system. Just before the harvest we would adjourn our club dinner and meet at the various plantations, walk over the crop, and dine at our various winter residences on the river. Then would we have swell dinners, when all the good things from the plantation and sea-shore were served in grand style. These meetings did much good, for they brought all the planters together and so kept up that social intercourse which formal visiting could not have done, inasmuch as we would never spare time for such. On the first of November, all moved from our summer homes and lived on the plantations. Of course there was much to be looked after then, but we all had more time, the crop was harvested and had only to be prepared for market. . . .

The social life on Waccamaw in winter was most pleasant; visiting, dinner, and evening parties brought us nearer together, and there was a nameless charm which pervaded the atmosphere around where a planter existed which rendered it in many ways very fascinating. The life of a well born and well educated planter—I mean by this, an owner, master or mistress, of a large number of negroes—was surely not one of indolence or self-indulgence. Apart from the mere welfare of those who belonged to him and those viewing the question as purely mercenary, an interest was taken in all that appertained to their domestic life. Remember this life was not in his (the Master's) hand, but all else most assuredly was: his [the negro's] home and its surroundings, his marital relations, the comfort of his wife and children and that of the parents of the same, when old age rendered them a care, the religious instruction of adults and children, and all matters where humanity and generosity were to be exercised. The owner had a vast deal to occupy his thoughts and time.

Of course, there were brutish owners just as there were vicious parents all over the world. These were the exceptions. No home on earth was as safe as that on a plantation where the negroes outnumbered the whites from ten to twenty times. The doors generally were unlocked at night. Of course petty thefts occurred, but murder, arson, and all the long list of horrible crimes were unknown. There was no need of penitentiaries, as far as the negro was concerned, and, indeed, crime among the white race was immeasureably below what it is now, when thirty years of freedom has developed crime to such an alarming extent. The master of a large plantation would leave wife and children and all he held dear on earth in the hands of his negroes, and absent himself for weeks and months with less apprehension than he now would in a city whose municipal regulations were presumed to be of the very best. To leave a family now on a farm or plantation would be simply madness. It is quite impossible to build penitentiaries large enough to hold all criminals, save at an enormous cost. . . .

I have told you of my summer life in my little Cottage by the Sea. My horses and vehicles were kept across the creek on the main land in order that I could leave at any time of tide, for when it was high water the creeks were too deep for crossing. A servant always awaited my return. . . .

The two largest crops of rice which I had ever made were under the most adverse circumstances. This doubtless evinces much egotism but if "self-praise goes but little ways" the money which these two crops yielded went a long way to purchase indemnity for the same. [The year] 1845 was known as the "great salt-water year." Little or no rain had fallen in the Up Country, so that the rice rivers became very low, and consequently the salt water gradually flowed higher up the rivers than the oldest inhabitants could remember. Woodbourne had only begun to be cleared, and I was attending to my father's planting interests at Weehawka and True Blue. The young rice was up on 600 acres of land and looked finely, but the planters were apprehensive about the continued advances of the salt water. The crop did not need water, but the question was, what was to be done if no fresh water could be had within the next two weeks, when the rice would die if not watered. The overseer came to me in great tribulation and begged that I would relieve him of all responsibility. Now this meant the loss of thirty to forty thousand dollars which was to be shifted from his shoulders on mine.

For me to have given orders contrary to his, when so much was at stake, would have been unwise. But now I had to act promptly, which I did; but not before I made him state in the presence of a witness that he considered the crop as lost. I called the trunk minders and told them to take on the water night and day, on all the fields;

to take a piece of soap in their pockets, and as soon as the same would not lather, to shut off the water till the next tide, and so filling the fields with water only at half tide, before the high tide brought up the water from the ocean. The rice did not need water for two weeks and to put it on now was against all rule, but to me it was rule and ruin. The overseer grinned when he heard the orders and said "Well, now the crop is lost totally." My uncle Dr. Smith was standing by, and said to me, "Don't assume such a responsibility." I said to him, "I know just what I am doing, don't worry about it," and the only consolation I got was in the alacrity with which the trunk minders received their orders and carried out the same. I could see at a glance that they approved and would stand night and day at their work if only to prove that I was right. Ah! The old-time negro was a great institution, and we ne'er will see his like again.

And here let me digress from the crop subject and say that two summers after, one of these same trunk minders fell on the river bank in an apoplectic fit, and when I reached Weehawka the overseer told me that poor Stephen was dying of apoplexy; and how I ran my horse to the home and rushed into the library to find a physician's *vade mecum*—not to diagnose the case, but for the remedy—and how I flew back, pulled my coat off, and worked on and for the patient, bled, physicked and all I could, till I restored him to consciousness; and when the doctor came [I] was rewarded by hearing him say that I had saved his life. I felt then that I was born to be a physician and doubtless could stand next to Sir Ashley Cooper. Well, Stephen got well; he saved my crop by following orders, and I his life, by the same process.

But I must return to a most interesting event. By taking in water at the half tide, I filled, in time, every field on the two plantations with fresh water. I cut the cross banks, because the water in the creek was already becoming brackish, and by this means let the fresh water flow from one field to another. The young rice could just be seen above the water. I then had the trunk nailed down and awaited the issue. I need not say that I *was* anxious, but each day made me less so, for the salt water came up the river till it was as salt as the ocean. Sea fish could be seen and even porpoises on the river. All the green sedge, etc., on the banks was killed and was as brown as December. All the crops below and above were lost or partially so, for not one drop of water could be had and no rain fell. My 600 acres was an oasis in the desert around me. The fun of the thing was that there was really nothing for the negroes to do. As soon as I found that there was no chance of a change, I had the flats ready and sent all of my father's negroes to Woodbourne to assist mine in clearing land. All things seemed to work for my good this season. I had lots of land cleared on my own plantation, whilst I watched carefully my father's crop which was being made without work, for from June till I had the water drawn off in the end of August, to harvest the crop, nothing was done, but to see the rice grow. I would walk around the fields daily and each day made things look and feel better.

An amusing incident happened one day on one of my walks. Rice banks are narrow and one has to walk ahead of the other. The overseer always walked behind. We came to where the water had run over one of the cross banks, say to seventy five yards. Now it was unsafe for one to get his feet wet in summer on the rice fields; fever usually followed such imprudence. So I said to the overseer, a great raw boned fellow of six feet, "There is really no use for both of us to wade through this water, if you will jump on my back I will carry you over." I could not have held him for one second for he was a 200 pounder. He looked at me and laughed at my innocence and said, "You don't think I would trust myself on your back; so jump on mine and I will 'tote' you safely." I confess, I was just a little dubious for fear he would *accidentally* stumble on purpose and dump some of the cheek out of me. But no, he landed me safely. When someone mentioned it at Club there was no end to the jokes against me. "Confound the boy, he thinks because he has saved his crop, he must need ride the overseer around." Well, such a crop on 600 acres never grew on the river before; sixty-five bushels and over was made to the acre on the 600 acres, and worth $1.00 per bushel in the rough. . . . I will here state that the Waccamaw did not yield, as largely to the acre, as the Savannah, but the rice was heavier and brought much better prices.

And now whilst I am in a bragging mood I will anticipate several years of my life and tell how I saved a crop on my own plantation, Woodbourne. My heavy work was over, there. Four hundred and fifty acres of first class rice land had been reclaimed from river and forest. All was one mass of beautiful rice in August, when I learned that a heavy freshet was coming down the Peedee. This was long before the signal service gave timely warning of dangers ahead, but after that when the seers told of impending evil, so one had to trust to his own sagacity. The Waccamaw river was very low. I knew that as soon as the former would reach my place, which was a peninsula between the two rivers, it would flow across my fields and find its level on the Waccamaw. The crop was a splendid one, just "heading out" and if over-toppled by water, would be blasted. Now the rice was high enough to keep its head above the water, but if the Peedee rushed across to the other lower river the force of the water would throw the plant down and so knock me out of about $15,000.

I was ill on Pawley's Island, with country fever, but I crawled out of bed at 3 o'clock A.M., and before the family (for I was married then) knew of my intentions I was on my way to Woodbourne, sixteen miles away. I nearly fainted when I reached the plantation but went at once to the house and sent for my overseer and gave him full instructions. I told him I would send him a barrel of coffee and one of sugar for the hands, and to work them day and night, one half to sleep, while the other worked. That the head bank which was only 150 yards long must be raised with sand, which was near by, till the water began to fall. Sand will resist water when not rushing and only rising slowly. Often the water began to trickle over the bank but large trunks of sand would prevent a break, and so for a while was the fight made, and a bank, say, [originally] about four feet high was ten feet when the water subsided. And so the crop was saved, and sixty bushels of rice per acre made. Had this plan not been formulated and executed, not one bushel of rice would have been made; and the overseer never would have thought of what I had ordered. The loss in my neighborhood was great. . . .

I went home that night and was ill for two weeks, but I would have been anyway, and I felt compensated. I would not let your sweet grandmother send for a doctor, and told her one day that I was better and got out of bed; then I fainted and had the mortification to see when I revived, by my side not only a doctor but a parson—neither of which was acceptable to me just then. The application of these two incidents is simply this: in an emergency make up your mind quickly as to what is to be done and do it. Do not consult about it, but take the credit or the blame. Again I have traveled far ahead of time, for this latter incident happened after Woodbourne was fully equipped and settled.

My father had now concluded to return to True Blue in the winter months and so I built a two room house on the banks of the river Bull Creek, so that I could attend more closely to the clearing of my land, etc. It was only weather-boarded and not plastered, with a shed in front—a pretty rough domicile in a grove of live and water oaks about 100 yards from the river and a mile and a half from where my negroes and overseer lived. . . . It did not take long to knock up my shanty, and when finished, I made a raid on my father's house for suitable furniture. In the dining-room I had a huge mahogany sideboard—which used to belong to my Uncle Tom and doubtless had seen service—which consumed a large portion of the room, and an oval dining table appropriated all the rest. . . . My bed-room had an elaborately carved high posted bedstead, etc. There were no out-buildings; no, not one. My servant Billy Gregg would cook my meals (he was then only 14 years of age) under the spreading branches of a live oak, and when it was ready and awaiting my coming, he would call my dog Casto to keep intruders off, whilst he set the table, not in motion, but in readiness. My little pony, Nick of the Woods . . . and a little dun cow kept each other company on the opposite side of a moss covered black jack. . . .

Sometimes my larder was beautifully supplied; and [now and] then I was on short rations. A deer would hang under the shed, which told of venison steaks, but I had no time for hunting and would only now and then bring home game which I had killed whilst roving through these dense swamps. I remember seeing a deer come within ten feet of the house, I presume from idle curiosity, and in the spring the wild turkeys would gobble all around where I was eating my solitary breakfast. Sometimes I would cross my pony over the river and go to True Blue for Sunday, but this was the only day of rest or companionship. In the summer I would remove to Pawley's Island and superintend Weehawka, True Blue, and Woodbourne. My investment was not considered a good one by any but myself. I was, of course, in debt, all going out and nothing coming in, as I have said I was now offered $20,000 for Woodbourne, which my father urged me to accept. . . . I told him I could not, as the sum would not pay for all I had purchased in negroes and the work done. . . .

In the winter I would sometimes go to Charleston and attend the races, being a member of the Jockey Club, and attend the balls given at this season of the year, etc.[8] But I was not long absent, and the wild life in the swamps had a fascination for me. The first day or two [it] was rather trying to a young man who had been driving his fancy team on the old Washington race course, to slip into his top-boots and corduroy shooting jacket and mount his little pony and ride to the nearest point where the hands were clearing and ditching, tie him to a tree, and plod through mud and briar day in and day out. But now I had to succeed, or be literally "swamped."

My friend Alexander Robertson stood squarely by me financially. . . . [He was] of the firm of Messrs. Robertson and Blacklock, rice-factors of Charleston, which previous to the Civil War was the largest in the City.[9] They were both cousins of my mother's and were very devoted friends of mine. (Mr. Robertson had been a clerk in the house of Kershaw and Lewis, rice-factors; my grandfather, as I have said, was a man of fine judgment, and told Mr. Kershaw that he wished him to take his clerk into partnership. Enormous quantities of rice were sent to the firm by the Alstons; so his wish was law, and the future firm was Kershaw, Lewis and Robertson.) When I returned from college and entered the profession of rice planting as naturally as a duck took to water, Mr. Robertson came to me and said, "your grandfather made me what I am, and I wish to return all his kindness to you." No man ever had a firmer friend that he. . . . Any amount of money I wanted in reason (from $1,000 to $20,000) I could have and no security asked. I never had a note in bank though I was at one time $45,000 in debt. I returned to them the last cent, and before the opening of the war we were all fairly

---

[8] [Irving], *The South Carolina Jockey Club,* p. 154, has this to say of the ball held in conjunction with the annual meeting of the Club: "The ball! . . . *par excellance* of *all* balls! . . . the chalked floors, the superb dresses of the company, the furbelows, the flounces, the bouquets of fresh rosebuds and camelias, the exhilarating music, the ceaseless whirl of muslin and of broadcloth . . . the handsome mirrors . . . reflecting graceful figures . . . lending enchantment to the brilliant scene."

[9] Easterby, *The South Carolina Rice Plantation,* confirms J. M. A.'s estimate of the firm of Robertson and Blacklock, with references and letters between R. F. W. Allston and Alexander Robertson, and explains the firm's name (p. 37). Robertson's summer home at Fletcher, N.C., is discussed in Brewster, *Summer Migrations and Resorts,* p. 69.

rich men; but, alas, in four years we were quite the reverse, they a little worse off than myself. Poor Robertson—I can never forget him. He died only a short time since, broken in fortune, a very old man, in Buncombe, North Carolina, his once lovely summer home where we drank the bottle of "[Luna] Madeira." When I visited Charleston alone, I would stay with one of the firm, where I was ever warmly welcomed.

But again I must retrace my steps. . . . My quasi solitary life in the cottage at Pawley's Island and wholly solitary one at Woodbourne for so long a time entitled me to a vacation. So after I had a good crop growing at my father's plantations, and had my first rice crop, on about 75 acres of my roughly prepared land at Woodbourne, where the rice was scratched into the soil among the stumps and roots, and the banks only one-half the required height, I prepared to leave for a season. Waccamaw, the Robinson Crusoe life I had led for so long, suddenly had lost all charms for me. Business seemed a bore, and even my deer-hounds would look imploringly, with their large intelligent eyes, to know why the sound of the horn never called them for the chase. . . .

I was going to Habersham County, Georgia, to pass some time with my father and shoot in the fall. An amusing little incident occurred on the evening before I left. I had sent my horses, etc., across the river and packed up all my household goods, intending to leave at sunrise next day. In the afternoon, whilst on my piazza on Pawley's Island, one by one the gentlemen began to drop in to say "goodbye," until some half a dozen assembled, laughing and talking as time wore on, and I began to feel uneasy, fearing they might conclude to stay to tea. My all had been sent off, and there was literally nothing in the house, and there was nothing to be done but watch and wait. Of course, they all intended to take tea with me—there was no mistake about it, and really I could make no excuses and did all I could to make their visit pleasant. Some came from the adjoining islands, and some refreshments should be set up by the host. Of course, I was more than pleased to see them, but the longer they remained, the more uncomfortable I became. I could not invite them to tea for I had none, cold or hot, in the dismantled house, nor could I offer an excuse before I knew whether they contemplated remaining. In this dire emergency out walked my servant Billy on the piazza, where we were all sitting, with a huge waiter containing a lovely array of dainty china, tea, coffee, cream, sugar. This was followed by another of muffins, cakes. The boy had seen the trouble, and had flown to a neighbor and told her (Mrs. John LaBruce) of his master's dilemma, and true to her ladylike instincts she busied herself in my behalf, and saved me a large amount of mortification. Now the best of the joke was that her husband was one of the party, and I feared he would put in a claim to the ownership of the whole, when he saw his name on the silver spoons, etc. Long after, I asked him if he had recognized his property. He said he had not, till in playing with his tea-spoon he saw his name thereon, and very nearly laughed out, but commended Billy for his astuteness in saving the reputation of the family, which by the way, consisted of his master and himself.

. . .

Early next morning I bade adieu to the Cottage by the Sea (little dreaming that I would never occupy it again) and to the rice fields where I had worked so persistently, crossed over the Waccamaw and Peedee rivers, to where my phaeton and horses awaited me. I made a straight shoot for Habersham County, Georgia, across the widest portion of South Carolina, a distance of several hundred miles, making only about thirty miles per day. I drove a fine pair of bob-tailed bay ponies, Bob and Badger, and had my Westley Richards double barrel, and my black setter Casto along; and as it was July the latter preferred to view the country from the phaeton, rather than on all fours. I would halt at midday and take my lunch under some shady tree and pass the night wherever I could find suitable quarters. I had left the rice fields behind me, and was taking my first *long* vacation. My first crop at Woodbourne had been planted and was looking well, though the banks were new and insecure. I physically needed a change and so enjoyed in anticipation the mountain breezes and fine hunting and shooting in the fall. Is it fortunate, or not, that we have a limited view of the future?

My crop was, a little later, swept away by an August freshet, not a bushel of rice gathered; and I don't think I even took my gun from its case; and, to be truthful, I never gave the loss of my crop a moment's consideration, and [I] had suddenly lost, also, all taste for field sports; for I had met a beautiful girl, the first sight of whose lovely form and face, had left no place in my heart and no hope on earth, save that of winning her. But I must go back to my journey—the crop had not *then* been lost and the heavenly vision had not *yet* appeared. I was still the young bachelor of twenty-seven, with little or no thought of the morrow, and with not the remotest idea of ever going heels over head in love. I was wedded to the work I had undertaken, and to secure a future thereby; and my pleasures were circumscribed to field sports—my horses and dogs, my rod and gun. If any one had told me that, ere long, a pack of hounds in full cry, the whirr of the ruffled-grouse from the mountain laurels, or the whiz of the reel in some shady trout stream, would not fascinate, I would surely have thought that he had lost his discriminating powers, or myself the eye and ear to nature's loveliest sights and sweetest sounds. But so it is, and it is well that we cannot look into the future. Anticipated pleasures would rob us of present peace, and despairing sorrows make us sigh for death.

The journey was without interest. I had never traveled over the country before and was often at a loss to know when I came to a fork which road to take. My servant never hesitated, and he knew less of the country than I did, for he was totally unaware in what direction Habersham County, Georgia, lay. I have often noticed the wonderful instinct, sagacity, or call it what you will, of the negro, in finding his way through the dense woods, even at night. . . .

My dog Casto was often much disgusted during the trip across the country, and it is very amusing to notice the reasoning powers of animals. I was sitting on the piazza, with the family with whom I was to spend the night. Of course Casto never for a moment lost sight of me and was sitting beside me when a wasp stung him on the nose, which so highly incensed him that he deliberately walked some distance to where the phaeton was, and jumped in and looked at me, as much as to say, "Come on and let us leave these rude people." The party were highly amused. But one night I heard a tremendous noise in my room and as soon as I could strike a light I found the dog barking furiously beside my bed. He had been sleeping by the fire place and the chimney board had fallen on him, which led him to think he had been attacked.

I have owned many setters and pointers, some very fine dogs of each breed. Upon the whole I think the pointer preferable. His short hair enables him to be kept cleaner, and he does not suffer from the heat in early fall shooting; he is more easily broken in and is not as headstrong as the setter, and when highly bred he shows off his graceful form. He suffers more from briars and becomes foot-sore more frequently, but upon the whole I prefer a well bred pointer. . . . On this trip I passed a night in Columbia, South Carolina, little dreaming that it was one day to be my future home, and where I expect to rest when "life's fitful fever is o'er."[10] I made a bee-line journey from Waccamaw to Ka-a, my father's summer home, pulled down the fences in the rear of the farm, and drove up to the back door, much to the amusement of the family. I remember asking my father what he bought *1,000* acres of land for, when fifty would have been ample. "Why," said he, "I don't like to hear my neighbor's dog bark." He expended far too much money on this place, at least $30,000, which yielded nothing but the pleasure of a country residence, and I often told him that all my work on the rice fields was spent here. But he was liberal in all things. I will here say that after the war Ka-a sold for $3,000, a loss of $27,000. During my father's residence here I attended to all his planting and interests on Waccamaw, and it was during this period that I received so many affectionate letters from him. . . .

Habersham County, around Clarksville, was quite a swell place in the days I write of. A number of families of note resided here during the summer on account of the fine climate and beautiful scenery. . . . During this summer (1847) I remember being at a large ball given by General Clinch, when the news came that his son-in-law, Robert Anderson, had been severely wounded in Mexico and was not expected to live. Of course this put an end to a very interesting party. But Anderson lived to take a most conspicuous part in his defense of Fort Sumter against the Confederates under Beauregard.[11]

. . .

My father's residence was seven miles from the village of Clarksville, and almost daily I would ride in to see the people and hear the news. One day while sitting on the veranda of the hotel I saw a party of young people pass by on their way to the bowling alley; among them was the beautiful girl I have alluded to. I did not then know her name, but I was deeply impressed with her grace and beauty, and to be introduced did not consume the period of a thousand years. I did not know if she was rich or poor, for I felt that my fate was sealed for weal or woe, and that life or death hung on the breath of this

[10] Mr. Alston, his wife, and several children are buried in Trinity church yard, Columbia, S.C.

[11] Every history of the United States has reference to Major Anderson. Wallace, *South Carolina: A Short History,* pp. 525 ff.

lovely girl.[12] I was not of a susceptible nature, and falling in love amounted to about the same thing as falling into the river, but I now discovered that they bore a close analogy, for in either case I had to sink or swim. . . .

Well, to epitomize a long story, I will only say that, as there were three aspirants, I had to see that I be not out-generaled. . . . What was most mortifying to my vanity, I was one morning informed by this sweet girl that she was going to Tallulah Falls for a week; that a party had been made up by a gentleman at his own expense, and that all expected to have a most pleasant time. I was now in a dilemma. I never went where I was not invited, but when I thought over the matter and discovered that one *devotee* had been invited and I left out, I felt that there was conspiracy in the air, the very breath of which was fatal to peace. Time now was precious—to me, it was worth its weight in pure gold. To join the party uninvited would never do, so I allowed it to settle down, when one morning I drove to the Falls; which was a public resort and only seven miles from Ka-a, and greeted the party with true politeness and told my servant to take my horses home, as I needed a little change of air. And so I had "nailed my colors to the mast." Well, I will write no more, for though it is now nearly forty-eight years ago, I feel the warm tears in my eyes as I recall the time and place. Suffice it to say that I was put in the same room with the fellows who had planned the picknick to my exclusion, and one night when they thought me fast asleep, I heard one say to the other, "Well, I fear it is all over with us." Poor fellow—he was killed leading his regiment into action in Virginia. . . .

I did not return from Tallulah as I went, empty handed, and anxious—but full of hope and of joy. What a change a day can bring forth. . . .

Of course the rest of the summer was a most delightful one, parties and picknicks being in order. . . . When the time came to

[12] The head stone at Mrs. Alston's grave in Trinity church yard reads: "Sacred to the memory of / Mary / The loving and beloved wife of J. Motte Alston / And daughter of the late Paul Fitzsimons / With exemplary fidelity and love / As daughter, wife and Mother / She faithfully performed all the duties of life / And on the 8th of April A. D. 1866, in the 36th year of her age / With an unwavering trust in God / She gently breathed that precious life away."

leave the mountains I drove a certain lovely girl in my phaeton to Athens, Georgia, where we spent several weeks, and then we went to to her home in Augusta, when I said adieu and returned to Waccamaw and my work at Woodbourne. As I have stated, my crop was lost and I was in the same predicament. . . . Heavy expenses had to be met and no rice to send to market. . . .

I had much to arrange. This was November and in February I was to be married. The loss of my entire crop was a sad inconvenience. The little bachelor retreat by the river side would never suit a bride. I had commenced to build a large residence on the Waccamaw side of my plantation but it was far from completion, and on whatever side I looked difficulties had to be met, and overcome. But at that period of my life I never failed in what I undertook and I soon had matters running more smoothly. I made several trips to Charleston and one or two to Augusta, but I pushed my plantation affairs on and into shape. The banks had to [be] raised very much higher to secure the crop from freshets, and, as there was no rice made, the long period of threshing was dispensed with.

In Charleston I bought a fine pair of dappled greys—bob-tailed and high steppers—Ajax and Mornus, and then bade adieu to my bachelor days in old Waccamaw, and with some members of my family I went to Augusta. My father and sister were met at the depot and taken to the Fitzsimons residence on Telfair Street, and I to Mrs. Hall's, where I had been accustomed to stop on my visits to Augusta. Etiquette required that I should not call that evening. But after dark I walked to the house and told the servant to tell his young mistress that I was in the dining room and, though forty-seven years have passed away, every feature of that lovely face and every movement of that graceful form that came stealthily and reproachfully into the room to greet me is fixed indelibly on my memory and can never be obliterated till the consummation of all is realized, when I shall meet her again in that spirit land which is so far off and yet so near.

The rain poured down all night, and when I went to the window of my room it still fell in torrents and the outlook seemed desperate. The wedding was to have been at Church at noon and a reception at the house, but the rain fell in one sheet of water and all was chaos and confusion. Weddings are not usually postponed, and after consultation the marriage took place at home where only a few attended.

The disappointment to many was great; but it was a matter of perfect indifference to me if it rained for "forty days and forty nights," for I knew that when the waters subsided that blessed "emblem of peace" would still be near me, and my hitherto half submerged life would now rise to purer and holier things.

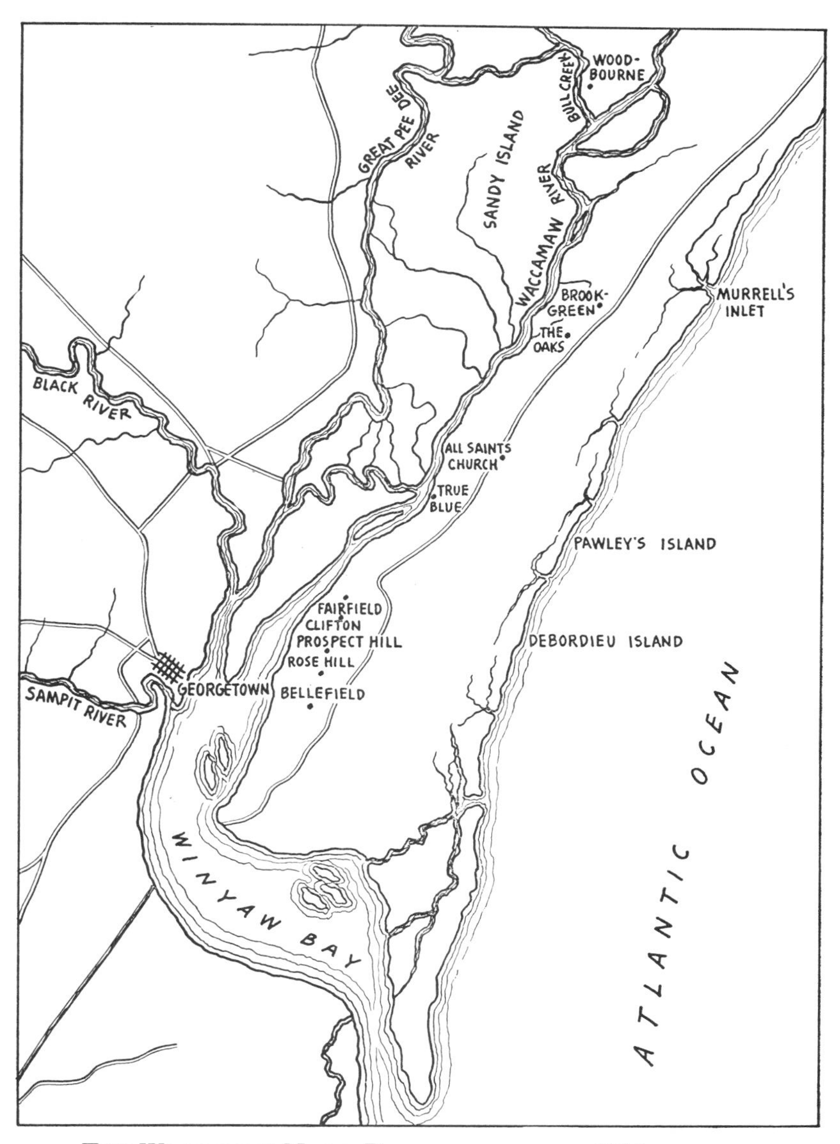

THE WACCAMAW NECK. REPRODUCED FROM 1953 EDITION.

William Alston of Clifton (1757–1839). Portrait by Thomas Sully. Courtesy of the Gibbes Museum of Art/Carolina Art Association, Charleston.

Mrs. William Alston of Clifton (Mary Brewton Motte, 1769–1838). Miniature by Charles Fraser. Courtesy of the Gibbes Museum of Art/Carolina Art Association, Charleston.

Old Rice Mill at Fairfield Plantation. Courtesy of the South Carolina Historical Society, Charleston.

Motte Alston Read (1872–1920) at Harvard, seated in the window. Courtesy of the Gibbes Museum of Art/Carolina Art Association, Charleston.

3

The Sportsman

All Saints Parish, Waccamaw, . . . is a neck of land some three miles wide with the ocean on the east and river on the west; the latter runs parallel to the former. From its position one can readily imagine what an abundant country it was; game of all kinds, deer, wild turkeys, ducks, etc., salt and fresh water fish, and all that the sea shore afforded.[1] The rice fields attracted millions of ducks. On most of the large plantations one of the negroes had nothing else to do in winter but to shoot for the table, and daily brought in far more game than the family could consume. The black duck (dusky duck of Audubon), mallard, sprig-tail, bull-necks, summer duck, blue and green winged teal, red heads, and sometimes canvass backs.[2] (The canvass backs are no better South than the other varieties. The wild celery of the Chesapeake gives the peculiar flavor.) These birds fed on rice and so were fat and finely flavored. I have known a hundred killed at two discharges of a double barrelled gun, and I have seen thirty-three blue winged teal killed by one discharge from a musket. Snipe and partridges were in abundance and woodcock at times. The latter I have looked upon as the gamest of birds; I mean the most enticing game bird to a sportsman; the

[1] A reader who is interested in further description of the fauna of the South Carolina Low Country may consult several chapters in James Henry Rice, Jr., *Glories of the Carolina Coast* (Columbia, 1925) and in its sequel, *The Aftermath of Glory* (Charleston, 1934). Also of interest to the naturalist and sportsman are the numerous works of Archibald Rutledge, among which might be mentioned *Plantation Game Trails* (New York, 1927), *An American Hunter* (New York, 1937), and *Hunter's Choice* (New York, 1946). An account by a contemporary of Alston's, William Elliott, *Carolina Sports by Land and Water* (3d ed.; Columbia, 1918), is also worth consulting.

[2] Alexander Sprunt, Jr., and E. Burnham Chamberlain, *South Carolina Bird Life* (Columbia, 1949), pp. 124-48, lists all of these ducks with the exception of "bull-necks." Possibly J. M. A. means the Ring-necked Duck, sometimes called "Bullhead." *Ibid.*, pp. 131-33.

peculiar whistle of his wings as he rises, the beautifully expressive eye and the soft, lovely brown plumage was ever most attractive to me, and on my tramps, of over fifty years, I would abandon all other game for the beautiful woodcock.

The bob-o-link would come in the spring to rob the fields of the newly sown rice. He would then be clothed in his gayest attire, black, buff, and brown, and from the topmost branches of the trees, or perched on the long reeds which fringed the rice field banks, you would hear his clearly defined notes; "bob-o-link -link -link," when making ready to renew his repast. These little fellows would ruin the "stand" of rice if not frightened away, so negro boys [were placed in the field] with long whips made of the inner bark of the hickory plaited into a long thong of some fifteen feet, and a short handle of only two feet would be swung around, when with a quick jerk a report would follow which was fully as loud as the report of a musquet.

When the rice was well out of the ground these little birds would take their first flight northward, and pillage on the wheat fields and finally settle down to domestic life in Pennsylvania and further North, and so reinforce their army as to be ready for their return South early in September, so as to be in time for the rice, two weeks, or more, before it was ready for the rice-hooks, just when it was in "milk." Each grain when squeezed, of course, would be blasted. Then these birds would come in myriads and in flocks so dense as to cast a shadow on the green and golden fields just bending with the long ears of grain. Now the males had doffed their black and buff attire and wore the livery of the female. And now was the time of action if the crop was not to be ruined. Musquets and double-barrels were brought into use to reinforce the long whips, shouting and hallowing, and every imaginable racket, to frighten off these little rascals, who would often swoop down, within twenty yards of you, and get a bite before scared off or slaughtered. Fine mustard-seed shot was used and hundreds were killed.[3]

---

[3] "The Bobolink . . . was received with anything but cordiality in the Carolina Low-country during the last century. It was, in fact, a very destructive form of avian life, one of the few birds which have merited such a characterization. . . . The Ricebirds were responsible for the loss of millions of dollars. . . . The specific name of this species, the Latin *oryzivorous,* means "rice-eating," and few birds have ever been better named." *Ibid.,* p. 489.

Nothing is more delicate than these birds, so fat [for] one thing, that when picked they looked like balls of yellow butter, not one particle of flesh to be seen. Delmonico, with all his art, could not produce a more delicate dish for breakfast than one of ricebirds in September. Two or three dozen [were] simply cooked in a frying pan—no lard, no butter, seasoned only with a little salt. Their own fat makes a dish full of yellow gravy, which with some Carolina "small rice" ("small rice" is the eye of the grain, which being smaller falls through the seive, after being pounded) affords a repast which would inspire one to write love verses though his nature be prosy in the extreme.

But the rice is now ready for the sickle, and our sweet little robbers are off for the everglades of Florida, where they, like some fashionable people now-a-days, pass the winter months. They now are called "rice-birds." On their return, as I have said, in the spring, they have donned their more sandy attire and are called "May-birds"—or "bob-o-links." On the marshes near Philadelphia, where numbers are killed for market, in the market in the fall they go by the name of "reed-birds."

I have kept these little fellows in a cage and noticed their change of plumage, and I remember as a boy on Debordieu I have heard my little prisoners answer to the call of their fellows, as high up in the air, on some clear moonlit night, they recognized far away the clear "tweet, tweet, tweet," as they winged their way from the marshes of the Delaware to revel on the pendant grain which now covered the fertile rice fields of Carolina and Georgia. Alas, most of these valuable lands have grown up into "bush" and doubtless our little rice birds are as much disgusted as the rice planters. I wonder if my little captives when I opened the door of their cage, to let them join their companions, told them how well I had treated them as little slaves.

The game, once so bountiful, is fast disappearing for various causes. The negroes previous to the war were not permitted to kill the same for market, and so there was no visible decrease. But even the sea birds—curlews, sea snipe, etc.—that used to be so abundant have dwindled away in Carolina.[4]

---

[4] The White Ibis, known locally as the Curlew, is making a return in South Carolina, J. M. A.'s Waccamaw area being considered its northern limit. *Ibid.*, pp. 100-1. By "sea snipe" Mr. Alston probably means the Eastern Dowitcher, known also as the Red-breasted, or Robin Snipe. *Ibid.*, pp. 245-46.

Ere I pass on to more rambling incidents I must tell how the rail is killed by the negroes, who call them "coots." Audubon, I think, names them "rail," or "lesser coot." After the rice has been harvested, the fields are covered with water, to the depth of a few inches, only enough to keep the stubble green, and sprout the grains of rice which have fallen during the harvest. These grains, if not sprouted during warm weather and so destroyed, germinate and grow with the crop rice grown in the spring as volunteer, and seriously injure the sales. The rail do not feed on rice, but live on grass seed, on which they become very fat. On dark nights the negroes, armed with bunches of long switches and torches of "fat lightwood" (resinous pine) with a large corn sack slung over their shoulders would go coot hunting. The birds would lie close till within a few feet of them and then fly up. When blinded by the bright light they would be gently switched down and safely deposited in the improvised game bag. Hundreds would be killed in a short time by these dusky pot-hunters, and numbers sold to the planters. I never was much "stuck" on rail, though so highly esteemed by many.

In the autumn the rice bird and the blue winged teal are by far the most dainty of all the good things which the rice fields yield. These last named birds at this season feed only on rice and as this grain is the most nutritious, they have a most delicate flavour. I remember in the long ago a guest of my father's was helped seven times at breakfast to one half of a blue winged teal each time. But they are tiny ducks, and in reality the breakfast was by no means a large one though three and a half ducks does sound pretty loud. They are easily killed when on the water; a low whistle makes them huddle together with their heads raised, when one discharge lays low a large number of these graceful little birds. In our barn yard when the rice was all stacked, before threshing, and where the poultry were allowed to run and feed ad libitum, they always had a finer flavour than those raised elsewhere. . . . They were as full-breasted as the ruffed grouse and far more juicy and excellent. . . .

Rice, too, when properly cooked is the best cereal for man; by far the most wholesome and nutritious. . . . Even the most accomplished cooks fail miserably. The old negro women on the rice fields cook this grain to perfection. Uncover, as you walk along the banks of the fields, one of their little three legged iron pots with its wooden cover, and try, if only from curiosity, the rice which they have prepared for their midday meal—boiled till *done,* the water "dreened" (drained) off, and set on the ashes to "soak." Around the pot there is a brown rice-cake, in the centre of which are the snow-white grains, each thoroughly done and each separate. Unless one has eaten rice cooked in this way, he knows nothing about it. The stuff called rice—soft and gluey—may do to paper a wall, but not to feed civilized man. . . .

But let me here change the subject, and as I have alluded to duck shooting, I will now attempt to describe what I considered by far the most enjoyable method of obtaining the greatest amount of sport out of this most interesting pastime.

I have never shot duck on the Chesapeake, where a large water-tight "box" [is] built very deep and weighted down so as only to show a narrow rim above the water, in which one or two shooters conceal themselves, . . . where the ducks fly from one point to another and are recovered when killed by small retrievers. Nor have I ever attempted the other method on the shores of the same Bay, where the shooter hides himself behind a "blind" and a trained dog of a breed peculiar to this portion of Maryland . . . is taught to run slowly to and fro on the bank or shore, which attracts the attention of the canvass back duck when swimming on the Chesapeake, and leads them from sheer curiosity to within gun shot of the sportsman. . . .

On the rice fields of Carolina the ducks come in vast numbers as soon as cool weather sets in. The beautiful summer or "wood duck" alone breeds here—all the other kinds are migratory.[5] This lovely little bird builds, or rather finds, its nest in the hollow of some tree near the river or creek, and has only to furnish some soft feathers from her own downy breast to make the above comfortable and safe during the period of incubation. As soon as the little yellow ducklings are well out of the shell they are tenderly lifted by the parent bird in their bills and are conveyed to the nearest water course, where they swim and dive with wonderful agility, and show themselves to "the manor born," as soon as they are placed where they can paddle their own canoe. I have seen a brood of these tiny little fellows, not much larger than the shells out of which they had so recently escaped,

[5] Modern ornithology confirms J. M. A.'s observation. The Wood Duck "is the only wild duck that breeds regularly in South Carolina." *Ibid.,* p. 126.

breasting the waves, . . . looking like tiny balls of yellow floss, their bright little eyes wide awake to danger, as they saw my canoe approach them, dive and rise again to the surface out of reach, having been apparently thoroughly instructed by their parents, or by nature, in a few days' tuition to beware of the treachery of man. How do these little atoms of creation become so knowing in the wiles of the world and dive to escape from a small boat when a log of equal size floating down with the tide would be unnoticed? Is this what we call instinct, or does the parent bird, afar off, guide her tender off-spring by some method of telepathy? . . .

My pony, Nick of the Woods, is at the door and my shooting jacket filled, not with shells, but with elastic wads and water-proof percussion caps; for the breech loading guns were in the future and we had only emerged from the days of the old "flint and steel," and the "percussion capped muzzle loader" was then the acme of perfection. (I carry the powder flask, and grass hopper spring shot powder and my Westly Richards double barrel, loaded with No. 5—for I always used for hunting or bird-shooting shot of one size smaller than usual.) To ride across the plantation to the Bull Creek, hardly a mile away, I hitch my pony, and find in a little creek which flows into the river, my canoe ready manned awaiting me. The little craft is thirteen feet long by two and a half feet wide, double headed, so as to move each way with ease and celerity. It is built of white cypress, and out of a single stick three-fourths of an inch thick and very light; and does not leak a drop, and [is] painted as near the color of the water as possible. My man who paddles is an expert; he sits in one end and handles his paddle with ease and adroitness, for it is made so as not to make the slightest sound as the boat flies through the water. The handle is round and smooth and the blade wide with the edge so thin that its dip into the water, and exit from, is noiseless. The wild duck is very shy and its hearing wonderfully acute, and the striking of the paddle on the side of the boat would put an end to all sport for the time being, the still water being a great conductor of sound.

We push out of the creek into the river and I land for a little while on the opposite side on Yahanee Island. This is an island of about 1,000 acres in extent, all of which is swamp land of primitive growth; through it wind long creeks with here and there lakes or, more properly "lagoons." The growth is of cypress, gum, ash, tupelo—huge vines and tangled brush and tall cane growing so close together that it is difficult to push your way through them. Before I enter one of these winding creeks, I land where I have had a little path, cut through the cane, which leads me to the head of Horseshoe lake by a short cut by land, rather than a longer distance by water. The cane grows thickest and fringes the edge of the lake. I have concealed myself here and seen the ducks swim so near to me that I felt it possible for me to stretch out my hand and yank one in. Here I would watch the drift of the birds on the water. If their heads were set the other way I would retrace my steps to my canoe, but if the flocks were drifting towards me, I had only to wait till I could put in two barrels with a fair amount of luck, not skill, for I confess this was what I always felt ashamed of, and what I deemed "pot-hunting." . . . The report of my gun brought my boat from where I had left it to the entrance of the lake on the opposite side and to where the dead birds lay, and the crippled ones could be recovered. I now resume my seat in the little canoe and commence my day's sport, for, as I have said, these first two shots did not come under that head.

We drift out of the lake and enter a long creek which empties into it and into the river. The tide is just right and is slowly running up stream, which makes it only necessary to guide the boat on the "off" or "near" side as the windings of the creek suggest, so that at every turn of the tortuous stream you come on the birds before they are aware of your presence. And here in the depths of the Carolina forest, which is alternately dry or wet, according to the state of the tide, no sound is heard save the chattering of the little squirrels as they so gracefully course along the tree tops, or the rapid tapping of the large black and white wood peckers, whose strokes on some hollow limb sound as if a large watchman's rattle had been sprung to warn the unwary but beautiful birds. . . . In the depths of these swamps the stillness is profound, where even the large brown owl is cheated by the gloom (when the sun is obscured) and hoots in anticipation. . . .

At each turn of the creek then do we expect to find our game, and experience had taught me as soon as the ducks were seen, in what direction they would fly. The mallards would almost invariably go to the right or left; the large black duck, or more properly, the "dusky-duck" of Audubon, in nine times out of ten, would make for the river and so give the shooter a double chance—one as they flew towards, and again as soon as they had passed overhead. The latter was the surest shot; for, as they rapidly approach you, only to shoot them in the head or to wing them will bring them down, for their thick coat of breast feathers usually causes the shot to glance. The little wood duck always flies from you, up or down stream as the case may be; and so the sport is continued till the head of the stream is reached and the same method pursued till we come to the river again. The game is picked up from the boat by hand. I sometimes would bring my retriever, but the noise he would make would lose me more shots than the winged birds he would recover. The little blue-winged teal I would seldom find in these wild retreats; he would frequent the flowed rice fields or the creek adjacent. Nor have I ever killed a sprig-tail or red-head or bull-neck in these secluded places, which is the home of the wood-duck. . . .

Now and then on these duck shootings I would get a wild turkey as he flew across the river;[6] and would by accident frighten up a deer, but he was as unprepared to see me as I was to salute him, and so would measure the distance between us, as, with his white tail, he bounded over the thick brush and, what was far worse, would disturb the game I was in quest of. I never made a record of my shooting, for sportsmen pull such long bows. . . . There is a tradition that a gentlemen on Peedee killed 100 ducks by two discharges of a doubled gun, i. e., four shots. My brother John brought home at True Blue eighty ducks by the same number of shots, and on visiting the pond next day he found about twenty more. . . . John was a keen sportsman and a fine shot, and wonderful stories are told of his unerring aim in Kansas where he was a Captain of volunteers who served against the Jayhawkers.[7]

I never knew such an abundant country for game of various kinds. Of the fishing I will write later on, when the dog-wood is in bloom and the trees are beginning to be clothed in green, when the honeysuckle lends its fragrance to the air and the maple reddens in the early morning light. . . .

---

[6] Once abundant all over South Carolina, the Wild, or Eastern Turkey is now virtually restricted to J. M. A.'s Tidewater area. *Ibid.*, p. 188.

[7] In the guerilla warfare between the pro- and anti-slavery men in the Kansas territory following the passage of the Kansas-Nebraska Act of 1854, the anti-slavery forces were known as "Jayhawkers." Several hundred South Carolinians went to Kansas to join the pro-slavery irregulars. See Wallace, *South Carolina: A Short History,* p. 519.

There were two methods of hunting deer. To go alone or, what was far better, with one companion and one thoroughly well trained deer hound. The woods of the low countries have numerous branches of thick brush, say of about 100 yards wide, with a little stream of water trickling through them; here the deer are fond of lying. On each side are usually open pine lands. Sometimes a little bell is attached to the collar of the dog so as to know exactly where he is before the deer is "jumped." One hunter rides his trained horse, which will stand fire from the saddle without moving, on one side of the branch, and the other [hunter rides] on the side opposite—abreast of each other and somewhat in advance of the dog. When the game is jumped, each hunter rides as noiselessly as he can, for as soon as the deer is pressed he leaves the thick underbrush and makes for the opening on one side or the other and is knocked down by the more fortunate hunter. Should he escape, the dog is called off and the hunt is renewed after the same fashion. To follow one deer with one dog would not pay, for it would be a chase of many miles, perhaps only to run him eight or ten miles into the river or salt creek, or even into the ocean, where he would swim out of sight with only his nose out of water. If you had time and patience you could await his return to the beach, which in spite of the drift would be close-by where he entered. But this was never or seldom done as he had been heated by a long chase, and the venison would be flavourless and unfit for use. This is one of the surest and most sportsman-like methods when only one or two are concerned.

"Still hunting," when you go with a dog and creep [up] on the game, I never practiced; and firelight hunting, when you go out at night with one to carry a torch and the other to shoot the poor deer, as he gazes with his beautiful eyes rendered luminous by the bright light before him and so guiding the pot-hunters to send the fatal bullet into the admiring and unsuspecting victim, was a sport which I never attempted and which was a little worse than still hunting.[8] We all kept a pack of fine deer hounds, and beautiful animals they were, with their sagacious countenances and long pendant ears hanging eight or ten inches down and close to the head.

Often during the winter we would have regular deer hunts. Each of us would leave home at an early hour and meet at some appointed

[8] Elliott, *Carolina Sports by Land and Water*, pp. 218-31, describes "firelight hunting" of deer.

place; and each would be accompanied by his deer driver, armed only with a long whip, which could crack with a report almost equal to a rifle, and by his individual pack of hounds. The drivers would be usually dressed in some light colour and a red cap so as to be as conspicuous as possible. Thus we would sometimes have some fifty hounds and several drivers to control them. One of the hunters was chosen "Captain" of the hunt, and he would arrange just where each hunter was to stand, from which spot he was not to move. These stands were known to those who hunted frequently, as deer have usually certain runs and so these stands were at some point where the deer would run, if not diverted from it. Each hunter was placed some two or three hundred yards apart, so as not to be hit by some stray shot fired by an over-excited person. Whilst the party were being placed at their respective stands, the drivers had taken the hounds some two or three miles above and [they] were then chased in to jump the deer. Sometimes two or three deer were started, and then with the shouts of the drivers and the united cry of fifty dogs, each in his own peculiar tongue, and the cheering voices of the sable drivers, who kept up on fleet horses well behind the hounds, the excitement of those who expected the deer to pass their stands was altogether most painfully delightful. Some one or two were compelled to have one or two shots if they were on the alert. A deer when thus pressed would almost jump on a man if he was motionless, but the slightest movement would divert the course, and perhaps give the shot to his neighbor. If the deer was killed, of course, the hounds came to a halt, but if wounded or unhurt the drivers with their whips soon put an end to the chase which would have been ruinous to the day's sport. New stands were taken and new drives entered on, and so on till the slanting sun told that it was time to give up the hunt and return to where we had all been invited to dine, where fresh clothes for dinner, and fresh horses and vehicles for our return home, awaited us.

These hunting parties and social gatherings were most pleasant. Around the dinner table the hunt was fully discussed and many a hearty laugh enjoyed at the expense of anyone who had failed to embrace the opportunity of showing himself a keen sportsman when occasion presented itself. Sometimes the ladies of the household appeared at table, but usually it was a "stag" party, not in compliment to the hunt, for our stags are called "bucks."

There was an old man who lived near True Blue, who was a keen deer hunter, named Singleton. He was only what was called a "law screener"—that is, a white man who had to live where there were many negroes on a plantation on which the owner did not reside, nor have an overseer. Thus the old man had nothing to do; so he and I used to hunt together continually. I had only to sound my horn as I passed where he lived and wait till he joined me. I can see him now on his little marsh-tacky dressed in blue jeans, his long double-barreled gun in hand and horn around his neck and his well-trained mongrel dog at his heels. "Morning Marse Motte, gwine to take a drive?" "Yes, old man, what else did you think I came for?" "That's a fact—but I just lowed you be goin' a courting." "Dry up and come along." Well, we never consulted what drives to take, for we hunted so long together that it was intuitive, and so we jogged on till we came to some favourite branch where we would put our two dogs in and follow them on each side, as I have described. And we have had lots of sport in this way. The planters used to say that Motte and old Singleton knew the abiding place of every deer on Waccamaw, and they were not very far off the track.[9]

Sometimes we would lie down on the clean russet pine straw to rest our dogs when the old fellow would amuse me with some of his yarns and hunting scrapes, though in fact, I had more narrow escapes than he did, for at times going at full speed through the woods I had some hard falls in trying to cut a deer off from taking refuge in the broad waters of Winyah Bay. Then as the day wore on, [we would] place our game across our horses, behind us, and if only one, share evenly between us. I can see the old fellow now with his corn-cob pipe between his lips riding along on his marsh tacky.

So well do I remember seeing a beautiful snowy owl of great size slowly flying from one pine to another and when I jumped from my horse to shoot it, how the old man entreated me not to kill a white owl, that good luck would depart from me evermore, if I was guilty of such an indiscretion. As bad luck would have it the noise frightened

[9] Deer are still abundant in J. M. A.'s hunting ground. Recently, while driving along U.S. Highway 17, which crosses property once owned by Mr. Alston's grandfather, the editor spied a deer standing beside the historical marker that locates the site of Colonel William Alston's Clifton plantation.

the lovely bird away and so by saving its own life my own autonomy was preserved, much to the pleasure of my old companion.[10]

He was taken very ill and I would go to see him and sit by his bed and talk to him. He had vague views as to the future, and I am not quite sure whether my own were translucently clear; but I sent the Reverend Mr. Glennie to see him, and when I came next day, he smiled and said, "I saw the parson and we had quite a chat together, but the fact is he sat too long and tired me, Marse Motte. I don't know if I am going to 'peg out,' but I had just as well tell you what I have not before; when I am gone, if you will go to the 'round head' drive you will find two peg horned bucks that are there." Strange to say I there did kill one of this description. But the old man did not die then, he lived some months, but never hunted again.

. . .

In hunting deer, or shooting duck on these marshes, you had to rely on the sagacity of the little marsh-tackeys. These ponies are reared on these marshes, and I have seen colts, only a few days old, swimming behind their dams with all the assurance of veterans. No wonder then that they could be trusted to pilot you through these treacherous morasses, even when the tide had covered all traces of the little paths which wound around, and when two feet to the right or left would plunge you into a bog up to your horse's ears. Only throw your rein on your pony's neck and place your feet behind your saddle and trust implicitly to the little creature's greater intelligence in such matters. See him put his nose on a level with the water and walk in with perfect confidence; don't urge or check him, but let him have his own way, for there is no turning back; you are now deep in the little creek and then up on the marshes, but all under water and the little fellow's nose guides him aright. And—when you reach one of the little islands on which are fresh-water ponds where you have come to find some duck and so amuse yourself in shooting—if you will wait till the tide goes out and retrace your steps you will be more than astonished to see how sagacious your little pilot had been in guiding you, when one false step would have plunged you "heels over head" in the soft ooze.

---

[10] As J. M. A. suggests, the appearance of the Snowy Owl is a rarity in South Carolina. Sprunt and Chamberlain, *South Carolina Bird Life,* p. 305, lists ten recorded sightings. Mr. Alston's, hitherto unrecorded, follows three sightings by Audubon and thus appears to be the fourth recorded sighting in the state in point of time.

My father and self would have these little marsh tackey mares bred to thorough-bred horses, which would produce very fine saddle, or light draft horses. We would never handle them till two and a half years old, and would name them after the English winning horses, and so you would hear of Amato, Phosphorus etc., etc., figuring, not at the Derby, or St. Leger, but as hardy sure-footed roadsters, who had never seen corn till stabled. These marsh tackeys were the toughest and most enduring animals possible; their feet were as hard as flint and were never shod; and when properly broken they were gentle and kind. They all came from the Spanish, or Andalusian stock, which their color showed. Some of these horses were very small, but beautifully formed. Before the civil war there were large droves of them, called in North Carolina "surf ponies," and in South Carolina, "marsh tackeys." I presume there are few now left. Some of the Indians in the Indian Territory have yet this same breed of horses, which I presume were carried there from Carolina and Florida, for their shape and coloring is the same, as also their kindly disposition. They are sometimes shipped to the more eastern states and sold for high prices.

I promised to give you an account of fresh water fishing in the low country of Carolina.[11] . . . I will here jot down a fair account of the day's sport. Always bear in mind that we are now about to fish in tide water. This alone will show when not observed and heeded, where good or bad luck comes in, but there [is] another concomitant which will often prove that a lack of sport is simply a want of knowledge. The habits of the lower creation must be studied by man if he will be a successful sportsman.

The usual rise and fall of the tide, as high up the river as Woodbourne, some forty miles, varies according to "spring" and "neap" tides, also measurably as to east or west winds prevailing, and in a great degree as to the fullness of the river from rains higher up. All these things taken into consideration make a vast difference in the fisherman's luck. There is no use to go fishing when the wind and the water are not right, and don't smile when I whisper in your

[11] Philip A. Murray, Jr., *Fishing in the Carolinas* (Chapel Hill, N.C., 1941), a modern scientific account, shows the accuracy of Mr. Alston's descriptions of fresh-water fish. Readers who wish to pursue the subject further will find a number of related books listed in Chapter III of Mr. Murray's study.

ear, that *bright* moonlight nights give dull days for fishing. The reason is that the fish feed more than on dark nights and are consequently not so hungry and eager to strike at the cunningly baited hook.

But the horses are ready and we ride across from one river to the other, less than a mile, to where my double headed canoe awaits us. The rods, bait, and hooks are snugly stored away in the trim little craft by the man who is to take us across the river to the creek from which opens Horseshoe lake. The rods are of domestic growth and manufacture, for on these swamps grow long tapering cane, which when properly treated, makes tough, elastic rods. When first cut and stripped they are passed through hot ashes and at once hung up by their tips to some over hanging limb, with weights attached to each, and allowed to remain till partially dried and then rubbed down with sand paper and oiled. I always used a reel, if for no other purpose than to lengthen or shorten the fine silk line, amid the over-hanging branches which fringed the borders of the lakes and creeks.

The day is lovely, and as we shoot across the river the gentle flowing waters and fleecy clouds are good omens of a fine day for sport. Soon we reach the entrance of the long winding creeks, where branches of living green dip nearly into the still water on either side, in which the finny beauties love to shelter themselves when the rays of the sun throw too much light on these shady surroundings. As we enter the lake to the left not a ripple disturbs its glasslike surface, over which dart here and there, winged insects of various hues at which ever and anon some greedy trout will strike, only to find itself mistaken, for these swift little things will fly rapidly in one direction and in one-half second turn at an acute angle and so continue their zigzag flight, doubtless to the regret of some that would like to calculate accurately just when to make a successful strike.

The bream is one of, if not the finest pan fish in the world. He is about as broad as a man's hand, and a pretty large hand at that, and his length twice his breadth. There are several varieties; the "blue-bream" from his color, and the "copper-nose" which, also, has a dark red spot back of the eyes. They are very vigorous fish and pull harder than many fish of twice their size; they never nibble, but bite, if they are going to bite at all, rapidly and vigorously, and fight to the end. This is the season when they are bedding and if you could see clearly beneath the surface you would find them to the number of from ten to twenty swimming slowly in a circumscribed circle, and this of all others is the time and place to fill your basket with these fine fish. Our little shell of a boat, wide enough to be steady and light enough to move silently by the slightest dip of the broad but sharp edged paddle, moves without a ripple, for when these fish are bedding they are wonderfully shy. When fishing from the shore, I have had to hide behind a tree and cast my line noiselessly into the water, but now we keep well off from the shore, where even our shadows in the water will not disturb them, while the in-coming tide moves the boat almost imperceptibly along. A quick, strong pull and the elastic rod bends till its tip touches the water. See what a beauty he is, as the man who wields the paddles lifts him noiselessly from the surface of the water safely into the basket at his feet; another and another in quick succession, tell us that we have found a "bed"—i. e., where they spawn—and a cane sharpened at one end is quickly thrust into the soft bottom of the lake which holds the boat within easy throw of the lucky spot. To strike the boat, or speak above a whisper, would frighten these shy game fish away, and so we take them in rapidly and quietly till the few which are left doubtless dart away in quest of their missing companions. The sport has been fine, but there is no need to remain here longer, for in two hours you may not get another bite; and so we "bout ship" and head for the long winding creek in quest of other varieties.

The tide is still flowing slowly up stream, and it is only necessary to keep the canoe in the middle of the stream and cast on either side. Early in the morning, or late in the evening is the time for fishing, but in these secluded haunts when the over-hanging trees are in leaf, even at mid-day, a twilight hue is cast upon the profound stillness of the scene. All is so intensely quiet that our little crew seems to have caught the infection and do not speak for fear of breaking the spell which seems to have bound each one to his own thoughts. The huge vines of the wild grape, which climb to the tops of the tallest trees and hang in festoons over the water, are now in flower and fill the air with their fragrance; and the only sound that falls upon the ear is that of the droning bee as he flies to and fro, ladened with honey for its hive in the deep hollow of some gigantic cypress.

But we did not come here to expatiate on the beauties of nature, or paint with words those charms of solitude, "which sages have seen in thy face," but to try our luck with rod and line. Thus far we have been in the swim of luck, and now let us wake up to something equally enjoyable. And so, as we drift along, we pick up right and left some lovely specimens, a few more bream, huge old fellows who have been snapping at the little green flies, but who are now in turn snapped up by the art of man. Throw your line now near that old log and put on an extra bait to suit the taste of some old greedy Warmouth perch. There, you have him; he pulls well, but not with the life and spirit of the incomparable bream. See his dark scales, the goggle eyes, and the huge spines erect on his back. Yes, he is pretty fair pan fish, rather dry and not as flaky as the bream. And so we hit and miss by turn till it is time to retrace our course down stream. Reel up your lines and stow away the rods safely beside you, for they are not shop made and jointed (not that I ignore such by any means), for we shall need them again when we reach the mouth of the creek where it enters the river.

Now let me introduce to you a barbarous implement, and an unsportsmanlike pastime. We must reach home in time to have a fish dinner, for the sooner they are cooked the better; "out of the water into the fire" is the rule which is ever applied to fish by those who wish to enjoy a delicate repast. As we go down stream, I will take out what we called in years gone-by a bob, which is made of three fairly large hooks, the shanks of which are welded together, and to which is attached a strong short line of about two feet in length, which is tied to a rod of good length from which some two feet of the tip has been cut off in order to render it pretty stiff and strong. The hooks are concealed in the brown and white end of a deer's tail. The inventive genius of man had about this time substituted what is known as a "spoon" or "spinner," made of nickel plate, which closely resembles a little silver fish as it is made to spin through the water.

I use the bob with a fair amount of dexterity, making it dart about the favourite haunts of what we call in the low county of Carolina, the fresh water trout, which has a huge mouth and is sometimes two feet in length. He is a greedy fish, but at times very choice in the selection of what he strikes at; but when satisfied it is of the right kind he pitches into it head foremost, rapidly and fiercely, with his capacious mouth wide open. This fish is called in Virginia and some other states the black bass, of which there are two varieties, the large and small mouth black bass. The bob, today, does not seem to suit his taste, so I detach it from the end of the short line and substitute a brand new "spinner," silvery and bright, which now moves with cunning celerity close to some dark old cypress log, or root, which has for the last fifty years or more lain undisturbed in the same spot where it had fallen or grown; or perhaps the wary old fellow is using those large dark green leaves called "alligator tongues," which float on the surface as an umbrella, to shade his eyes. A fierce rush at the nimble little silvery spinner would set him down in these days as a "silverite," but not at the time of which I am writing, for we all then loved to feed with silver spoons, and some were doubtless taken in.[12] A tyro would have lost his head and so lost this superb fish, for the sudden rush on the surface of the calm water would have caused him to draw in quickly the tempting metallic bait and so deprive the fish of being taken in out of the net. After the strike there is no further sport for either fish or fisherman. Hand over hand the former is hauled into the boat, and the little "spinner" is again weaving meshes for unwary fish.

A fair amount of luck in the way of deception, which I would prefer not to call sport, brings us to where the creek empties into the river (Bull Creek). Here, where the water is deeper, we take up our rod and reel, but we now attach to our line a small float for we will try the beautiful Virginia perch, whose large size and bright silvery color makes him a great favourite with all true lovers of the rod and line. A small cord with a piece of lead or a stone will answer, attached and let down to the bottom [to] hold the tiny craft in place. Run up your float till about three feet of line is below the surface and be patient, but not silent unless it suits you. We have tried the bream when bedding where you fish on the bottom, and the trout with the artificial bait which spins on the surface; but now the fish we are after does not bite so greedily, nor so unwarily, and his habits, moreover, compel a middle course. A sportsman must learn the habits of all sorts of game, and even the pot hunter knows this to be true. This knowledge will nine times out of ten yield "good luck." Of course one will, or rather may, by accident stumble on a gold mine without being a geologist; so, also, may a gunner find a covey of

[12] Mr. Alston, writing in the 1890's, here indulges in a topical pun. In the controversy of that decade over the national monetary standard, supporters of the free coinage of silver were known as "silverites."

partridges and blazing away into them, on the ground, kill the last one at a single shot, without being a sportsman in any sense. . . .

Our little pretty colored floats are now bobbing up and down on the ripples caused by our proximity to the downward flowing river and whither our coveted silverites will turn in quest of food suitable to their cultivated taste. To meet which we have laid aside the earth worms (which every little boy is acquainted with from the time he used a bent pin for a hook), the uncanny catawba,[13] and the young wasp taken from its nest when white and succulent to a fish's taste, and now bait our Limerick with tiny minnows, which one or two dips of a little thread net as we floated along have transferred to a calabash or gourd, half filled with water to keep them lively. Keep your eye now on your float; for, look, it is under the water before you feel the bite; yes, you have him and a beauty he is—full ten inches long and six broad and as shiny as a brand new silver dollar ere dulled and tarnished by the hand of man and only kept valuable by the fiat of his government.

But really, it is time to go, if we are to have a fish dinner. The sun is on his western slant, and so we go after picking up a few more of these lovely fish, as specimens of what Bull Creek can do when appealed to by one who had passed some years on its sunny banks, and had learned full well when and how to ask favours of its ever flowing waters. Again we shoot across the river and up the little bayou where our horses so impatiently await us, for it is long past their dinner hour. Before we mount we look into our well filled basket, to admire a choice collection of some fine specimens of what the tide waters of Carolina can contribute to the lover of the rod and reel. We leave them now to the tender care of one who has done his part skillfully and faithfully in propelling our little boat. He knows full well what are required for the "house," and the rest, of course, fall to his share. Before they are brought home, they are carefully cleaned at the water's edge in order to avoid that operation in a heated kitchen.

But now to our rooms to get rid of our fishers' garments. . . . So come down into the dining room, for dinner is not ready, as we have to wait on the fish, and let me introduce you to the old time

---

[13] Known locally as "catawba" worms, the larvae of the catalpa moth make a favorite Carolina bait. The catalpa trees, on which the larvae feed, are known colloquially as "bait trees."

side board which used to grace my little shanty on the river side. . . . There were lots of drawers and shelves and doors; some of the former which were very narrow and deep and divided into little squares seemed to be made for decanters and bottles. . . . We will see what they contain. This old fashioned decanter holds some liquor of an unknown age. In drawing a bottle from my father's wine garret, at True Blue, I found, by accident, one of old Jamaica rum. . . . How long this bottle had played the gentleman, I have no idea, but I will testify to its taste from long association with such rich old wine. . . . This old bottle of Cognac was the "last of the Mohicans" and was doomed to live only in memory. These two ancient bottles doubtless could tell many an interesting anecdote of life's experiences, . . . one reared among the lovely vineyards of "la-belle-France," and the other which had breathed the soft air of the tropics, when the cane fields of Jamaica waved over one of the richest islands in the world. But we leave these old fellows undisturbed for the present, and ere we arise from the dinner table, a tiny glassful will be the medium of an expressive farewell. A glass of sherry now, and then to the parlour, where our lady friends await us.

But dinner is soon announced and let us see what Woodbourne can tempt us with. Remember always that we are nearly "out of humanity's reach,". . . . And so your lovely hostess will help you to some clam soup. Now I will venture to say you never tasted it served as that which is before you. It is prepared "a-la-Heriot," at whose hospitable board I first learned its rare excellence. Unless you had been reared and educated on the sea shore you would pronounce it turtle soup; but, no, it is concocted of the large clams of the Carolina coast which are reduced as fine as possible, and the flour used is browned, which gives it the appearance of turtle soup. . . . A couple of glasses of sherry and a tiny squeeze of lemon added are very far from being amiss.

But here are our blue breams, and if their color is changed, depend upon it, their presence is more than acceptable. Never place on the table a large dish of fine pan fish, for the delicate taste of those underneath is ruined by being smothered by the weight of those on top. Let them be introduced in pairs, in covered dishes, for by the time these are helped, another pair are on hand, and so on till the company is served to its content. They were lovely fellows when we whipped them into line, but they are infinitely larger now, or do they only appear so, when measured by a keen appetite? . . .

In the art of cooking I know I was never conceited, and few cared less for eating than I did; but, as I was in my day a keen sportsman, I never could bear to see game butchered by an ignorant cook. . . . You kill your deer in the chase, you shoot your bird on the wing, and so, I say it is a pity to see them come on the table so marred as scarcely to be recognized. Fine pan fish share this fate more frequently than others. Few cooks know how to, what is called, "fry a fish." They do really fry them, which renders them so indigestible. Their method is to put some lard into the frying-pan and when it begins to pop and fizzle and he has to shade his eyes with his hands to prevent the hot lard from putting them out, he blindly pitches in the poor fish which have made such a gallant fight for liberty, and removes them when so dry and hard that you could take them by the tips of the tails, and hold them at arm's length. This is the process of fish frying.

My cook was bound out for four years in Charleston to learn his "trade" as he called his profession, but the *art* he learned by experience. The fish put before you, believe me, were not treated as I have attempted to so *rigidly* portray, and the reason is obvious. When you attempt to cook fish "a-la-frying-pan," let your chef have as much pure leaf-lard, or sound fat bacon, as he desires. Melt the same, in that utensil which has served to fill the pockets of doctors and the graves of burial grounds—the frying-pan, and when *boiling* slip in your fish, after having been carefully washed and dried on a coarse, but scrupulously clean crash towel, and sprinkled with corn meal. The boiling hot liquid, so far from rendering the fish greasy, at once closes up the pores and excludes the liquid lard, and is simply cooked by the heat of of the same. When slightly brown, insert a two pronged fork, which will test, as to whether it is cooked sufficiently or not. . . .

Just let me give you a simple lesson, which will only take two minutes and will save you lots of trouble. See, I place the fish on a large plate, now remove the head and tail and the row of spines along the back, and here place your silver knife side ways and lift the upper side off. All the bones great and small are now exposed and are quickly removed and placed with the head, tail, and fins in a small plate near you, and taken off by the waiter. A little butter, salt and red pepper, if green peppers are not in season, and a squeeze of lemon ere you replace the two halves as you found them, minus the troublesome and dangerous bones. . . . I have ever looked with holy horror on them who pour vinegar on, or deluge a delicate fish or fowl with strong sauces which give all the same taste and effectually destroy the flavour of each. . . .

I felt secure so far as the bream were concerned, both in flavour and size. And now I prided myself on a brace of game fowls, a pair of pheasants, raised where they had a wide range and rough rice, ad libitum, to feed on, and sacrificed some days previously for man's enjoyment. These beautiful birds now appeared before us, of a dark brown color; their rounded breasts and long delicate feet gave them the appearance of their English cousins, some generations removed in kinship, but not in taste.[14] . . . Certainly these before us were artistically served, even though by the skill of one of the sons of "darkest Africa." Nothing could be more delicate, with only a suspicion of celery flavor, and a glass of good old sherry to induce another slice from the snow-white breast. . . .

In days gone by, the cloth was always removed, and the highly polished mahogany mirrowed the finely cut decanters and the delicate wine glasses. Here, when the ladies had retired, we would sit and discuss the topics of the way; be it rice planting or free trade. . . . Try, also, with your wine a few of these finest of all nuts, if they are the most common. They are before you nicely parched, shelled and cleared of the thin inner covering. We call them "ground-nuts"; at the North they are known as "pea-nuts"; and in Georgia, "Goobers," which last is the proper name, but not so spelled. This is an African nut and "Nguba" is according to travelers the proper mode of spelling and pronouncing this Americanized nut, but as it grows in the ground I don't see the use of going to Africa for a name. The flavour of this ground nut adds wonderfully to that of a glass of good old wine. . . .

---

[14] The Ruffed Grouse is commonly called "pheasant" in the Carolinas. See Sprunt and Chamberlain, *South Carolina Bird Life,* pp. 185-86. Efforts to introduce the Ring-necked Pheasant, the "English cousin" of which J. M. A. speaks, have not met with success. *Ibid.,* p. 557.

I was in Habersham County [in Georgia] where we were passing the summer, and a lovely home was Ka-a in those days. The society, as I have said before, was most select, the rides and drives charming, and the mountain scenery peculiarly beautiful. . . .

The partridge shooting in the fall was most enjoyable—to get out early in the morning when the air was cool and crisp and shoot till about ten and return with a bag of well grown birds to a late breakfast, when the appetite was as keen as the sport had been, and when all the senses had been sharpened by the lovely surroundings. I had a fine pointer, straw-colored, and of diminutive proportions. I could often trail the birds myself through the short dewy grass, and I remember so well, when "Zdenko" came to a point when the atmosphere was heavy, I could detect that peculiar odor which the covey gave out when alarmed at the near approach of the dog. Poor little birds, they had not been shot at long enough to learn the art of "withholding their scent." It is wonderful how cunning birds become—I have often seen them, particularly those which had been shot at, when they would alight on an open grass covered field, lie so close, their feathers so tightly pressed together, that the best dog would gallop over the artful little birds without coming to a point.

Some sportsmen deny that a bird has the faculty of "withholding its scent," but when the atmosphere is favourable, there is no doubt in my mind that this is often done, and a good dog scolded for what he did not deserve. Of course, a bird to accomplish this, never budges from where it alights. The training of pointers and setters is quite an art, and when one had a dog of fine temper and a good nose, and time enough to bestow on such a pastime, it was a pleasing task. Undue severity is objectionable, and kindness will accomplish what harshness often fails in. I once trained a setter which was terribly gun-shy and who as soon as the first shot was fired, would fly home and hide until my return. Such a dog had much better have been given away, or shot, but I wanted to see what kindness could accomplish; so I petted the coward, rendered so by some indiscretion, and thus made him trust implicitly in me. When he came to a point, he would tremble at the expectation of the dreaded report and so I would walk up to him and pat him and let the bird escape, in order to reassure him, till he would firmly stand and then drop instead of making haste to reach his own cover at home. I once owned a good dog who was afraid of thunder.

It was ever a great pleasure to sit on the fence and see a brace of well trained dogs gallop over the field and leave no portion but that was most carefully scrutinized, to watch so intelligently my hand as I would wave it in the direction I would have them go, to cross and re-cross each other, and so cover the whole field, and when one would come to a point, how quickly would the other recognize the fact by also coming to a stand even though far away and out of reach of the scent which his companion had discovered. It is quite remarkable how a dog with a dead bird in his mouth should scent another and come to a staunch point; one would suppose that with his nose buried in the one retrieved, he would fail to detect the fresh scent of another. But not so, I have seen a dog when leaping over a fence with a bird in his mouth, come to a point and never move from his position on the fence, awkward and uncomfortable as it was, when he recognized by his keen nose the presence of another bird, and this I have witnessed more than once. Of course, there are days when the fine nose of a well broken dog is at fault. In very dry or windy weather he is apt to blunder or perchance, even under the most favorable circumstances when the dog is all which could be wished for, your dog flunks his game, which may possibly be accounted for by his having had for his breakfast a tiny piece of "smoked herring." I have heard of this being done by way of a joke.

I remember once when shooting in Jefferson County, Georgia, in the piney woods; and after killing about fifty partridges when my companion and self should have bagged twice that number, we lost sight of our pointer dog. All the calling and whistling failed to discover his where-abouts, and so we concluded that he had chased a hare, and feeling ashamed of his conduct had determined not to come in and acknowledge his fault; when, after nearly an hour's fruitless search, we accidently stumbled upon him, curled up and fast asleep at the foot of a tree. He had trailed a covey of partridges for some distance and came to a point which no whistling could make him break, and being fagged out with a long day's shooting, he quietly crouched down and went to sleep. When we discovered him, he was apparently as much astonished as we were. The birds, in the meanwhile, had wandered off, but the dog soon struck the trail and staunchly pointed them some distance away, for our amusement, and their decimation. This seems a rather *tough* story, but it happened just as I have related it.

Rabun, the northeast county of Georgia, was only two or three miles from Ka-a and was the most picturesque portion of the state. It adjoined western North Carolina, which has been called the Switzerland of the United States. I would frequently hunt deer or shoot grouse in Rabun, and in the fall when the air was crisp and cool and the leaves had begun to turn to deep crimson and yellow, and all the various shades and tints between, it was certainly a most enchanting hunting ground. The whir of a pack of ruffled grouse—commonly called pheasants—as they arose from some secluded glen, where the stiff leaves of the kalmia coming in contact with the rapid wings of the row of frightened birds, would give forth a sound which was well calculated to unnerve, in some degree, even a well trained dog, to say nothing of the sportsman himself.

Often would I throw myself on the ground and revel in the lovely scenery: the clear blue sky above, and the mountains below, both far and near, so gorgeously attired; the call of the wild turkey to the flock from which he had been separated; the deep but musical tongue of the hound on his trail, now unexpectedly near and then afar off, as some sharp turn in the ravine below cut off the sound—all these sights and sounds come back most vividly, after so many years have passed away, which seemingly would have cut off all such trivial scenes from one's memory.

I can recall a bear hunt in Rabun on which occasion I do not think I displayed the courage which I should have owned. Not that I was at all alarmed at the possibility of being "hugged by the bar" but in quite another way. A party had gotten up the hunt; we were to camp out at night, in the mountains and though I never expected to see, hear, or smell Bruin I thought I could endure one night on the bare ground for his name sake and the company of a pleasant party. But a furious rain set in just as we had reached our camping ground, and as bear hunters do not usually supply themselves with umbrellas, we were what is styled, soaking wet, and the deep ravine which we had selected for our peaceful bivouac looked as disconsolate as our faces. The downpour came up so suddenly that there was no time allowed for any preparation.

All my courage was soon washed away, . . . when one of the party proposed that we should utilize the now swollen rivulet by trying our luck in fishing and began to unwind a tiny little line which he had brought along in case an opportunity should present itself by finding water enough in the mountains to wet it. I looked despairingly at my carefully loaded gun, as it leaned against a tree with the water bubbling out of the muzzle, and feeling that I would not be missed either by the party, or the bear, I concluded that I would take the "back track" and make for more comfortable quarters at Ka-a. The mountaineer, with whom I used to hunt, quietly said to me, "You will never reach home but will have to spend the night in a worse place than this." I only laughed when I mounted my little pony and galloped off.

The fierce storm had completely obliterated all signs of our trail and so to take the "back track" was an impossibility. All went fairly well for the first two miles, and all would have been well to the end could I have trusted to the horse-sense of the little beast I was riding. But he was a recent purchase and when I lost my reckoning and looked to him for guidance, as I had so often done, I felt that he would probably lead me deeper in the vastness of the mountains. The sun was obscured and the storm had changed the whole aspect of things, and I began to think that I had better have taken the wholesome advice of my mountain friend. To retrace my steps was as difficult as to push on, and just as I began to ponder what was to be done, I heard a shout and up rode Dover, the man I used to hunt with, and who had a hearty laugh at my predicament. "I knew just what would happen and that you would either break your neck, or be lost, so just mounted my bay, which is worth a dozen little blacks." He soon put me on the right trail, which I never would have found and he galloped back to the party I had deserted. Of course no bears were killed, which gave me a chance to "guy" the party by way of excusing the unsportsmanlike manner in which I had forsaken it as soon as I discovered that there was no sport by remaining. Is it not singular, or I should rather say suggestive, how trivial incidents of this kind are remembered. Having joined the party I should have stuck to it, and the present relief of getting rid of a miserable night on the wet ground, and the prospect of no sport to compensate for the same, was not a valid excuse for leaving. Conscience should ever be our guide in small, as well as great things, and the slightest departure from this ever present monitor's advice, never fails to recall our short-comings. . . .

Beyond Rabun was Western North Carolina, where I have passed nearly two years of my life. Cashier's Valley (why so called I never heard, certainly *not* because defaulting cashiers could enjoy so lovely a region, where money was so little thought of) is where the Hamptons and the Prestons had cottages for the summer months, where the climate was fine, the scenery grand, and the hunting so attractive. Even in July a huge hickory fire was necessary in the mornings and evenings, and two or three blankets not uncomfortable. Colonel Wade Hampton, the father of General Wade Hampton, stocked one of the streams here with the lovely little salmon trout. When I visited this valley they were not very plentiful, and after having rather poor luck, I swam out to a large rock in the stream, much to the amusement of the party, and from which place I caught one of these little beauties which was ten inches in length, which was far over the average. The deer hunting was good, for mountain hunting, which to me was never attractive, and quite too monotonous when compared to the same sport in the low country of Carolina. . . . The daughters of Colonel Hampton still make this valley their summer home. . . .[15]

I have had fine trout fishing in Tow River, at the foot of Mt. Mitchell. I remember while standing in the cold, swiftly running water of this stream when I thought that there was no one near, the tallest man I had ever seen appeared on the bank and said to me, "Stranger, you had best come out of that cold water, and fish from the bank, for you do not look strong enough to stand it." I told him that it amounted to the same, as I had to cross and re-cross so often. "Oh," said he, "I can fix that all right," and he walked in and putting one arm around me he put me on the bank as easily as I would a child. He was over seven feet and was highly pleased to see what was new to him, fly fishing, and remained with me all the time I fished, but would never let me go into the water, and then invited me to take dinner with him, which I was glad to do. A log hut with a clay floor was all he boasted of in the shape of a home. His wife cooked a most appetizing repast; fried chicken and ham, rich milk and crisp corn bread to a hungry fellow was far better than all Delmonico could furnish, particularly when the table and its contents were scrupulously clean. We parted good friends. He was afterwards a captain in the

[15] Brewster, *Summer Migrations and Resorts*, pp. 72-73, tells of the development of Cashier's Valley by the Hampton family.

Confederate army. When these mountain people take a fancy to you, they are most hospitable. . . .

When I reached Asheville, North Carolina, I mentioned what fine fishing I had had on Tow river, and one who was fond of this sport went over, but soon returned and told me that whilst fishing he heard the crack of a rifle, but did not pay any attention to it, until another report came and the ball struck a rock uncomfortably near him, which caused him to reel up his line and leave. These [mountain] people were ever jealous of a more enlightened, or better educated class settling among them. Prior to the war there was a settlement on the French Broad river, and the valley, which was from one to two miles broad, was put in the highest state of cultivation by planters from the low country of South Carolina, who built lovely cottages and passed the summer months there.[16] These were nearly all burned by the Tories; and these fine lands, produced sixty bushels of corn per acre, were offered for sale at $10.00. I wrote a firm in New York that these lands were the best investment I knew of. But, no, cotton was all the rage, and the French Broad was out of the "Cotton Belt." . . .

In a few years these lands commanded readily $100.00 per acre, and cotton lands could be bought for a song, and I may add, that the song of these cotton planters, and *they* who loaned them money, was one of sadness. I have some experience in this line myself, and if I live long enough to forget, in some slight degree, and have the courage to face again this portion of the uninviting past, I may trace on paper one of the experiences of life which I have ever tried to shut out. But I have again and again rambled off from where I tried to picture the many beauties of Habersham County, and . . . it is time to return to the low country of Carolina. . . .

[16] For these summer homes in the French Broad River valley and the South Carolinians who built them, see *ibid.*, pp. 63-71.

4

The Master of Woodbourne

It was in the early spring of 1848. I had been married only two weeks before, and we were on our way to Waccamaw, my father having sent his carriage to meet us in Charleston. . . . I had a nice lunch prepared in the City, and . . . our first repast was taken beneath the wide spreading branches of a huge live oak, which so vividly brought to mind my childhood days when traveling so often the same road with my grandparents. . . .

All, however, was extremely novel to one of the party, and it was most interesting to me to watch her countenance when so many unfamiliar objects met her view: the low-country of Carolina was new to her; the dense swamp foliage and tangled growth of huge vines of various kinds; the beautiful magnolias with their shining leaves, the festoons of yellow jessamine, now in full bloom, filling the atmosphere with its fragrance; old Georgetown with its antiquated buildings, sandy streets and rows of "China" trees; . . . and then the rice fields stretching away for forty miles. Crossing Black river, so called from the inky appearance of the water (the black hue of the water was caused by a dark coloured moss which covered the rocks in the bed of the river). The Indian name should not have been changed, for the "Weenee" was certainly more euphonious and just as suggestive to those who understood the Indian language. . . .

Our journey was nearly over. Having reached a point on the Peedee, opposite True Blue, one of my father's plantations, we met his eight oared boat to take us home, across the Peedee and Waccamaw rivers and through the winding creek connecting them. How amused I was at the admiration the oarsmen evinced as they gazed at their new young mistress, and how she smiled at their improvised boat songs, suitable to the occasion. The negro is a natural musician and has usually a fine voice, but it is only in the low countries of Carolina and Georgia that you hear them, on long trips up and down the rivers, improvise words suitable to the occasion and to the air. They are fond of the water and during the spring months when the windows are open their boat songs are peculiarly attractive in the still hours of the night.

From Charleston to Waccamaw we cross seven rivers, the Cooper, South and North Santee, Sampit, Black, Peedee, and Waccamaw. The last named six are near Georgetown, a thoroughly rice field region. Well, it only consumed an hour to reach home, the negroes bent to their oars and I soon stepped on the old familiar plantation, a man full of cares and responsibilities and of joys and delights which words were inadequate to express. It was not like coming among strangers, nor had I to introduce this more than fair girl to the family, for she had met them all at Ka-a; but I confess it was quite novel to me when I walked into the house with one who lent such a charm to the earth, the sea, the air, and far greater still, to my new life. . . .

One day my father proposed going up the river where my little bachelor box was built on the banks of Bull Creek, which as I have said, was the main branch of the Peedee. He was anxious to show his new daughter where and how I lived, so the eight oared boat was manned and taking advantage of the floodtide, we all started on a twenty mile row up the Waccamaw and the same distance back. We had boats on the river which were beautifully shaped, between 30 and 40 feet in length and over four feet in width, and sometimes built out of a single stick of cypress, but oftener of two. I have measured a tree on my plantation which was 22 feet in circumference.

At it was in the spring the river was peculiarly attractive; the cypress with its fringe-like-feathery foliage; the honey-suckle and fragrant bay-blossoms; the lilies floating near the banks; the common duck with his rich variegated plumage; the swallow skimming over the placid water; the inimitable mocking-bird—"the trick tongue" of the Indian—warbling his love song in the air, as he flew from tree to tree; the terrapins with their shiny backs and yellow under-shells sunning themselves on the logs; the sturgeon leaping out and turning a somersault as he splashed again into the water; the swiftly gliding boat impelled by willing oarsmen, singing to the even strokes of their long white oars—[all] was pleasant to the eye and ears of the voyagers and peculiarly novel to the fair girl who was making her first visit to her future home. One by one, the various plantation homes were coming into view, and then receding in the distance; the rice-fields just springing into life with their long rows of pale green, or still covered with the "sprout flow"; Sandy Island with its high hills of white sand, singularly barren, and yet surrounded with rice alluvial fields; and now *Woodbourne* in the distance, a long peninsula between the Waccamaw and Bull Creek, the waters of the former black and those of the latter clay-coloured, which flow a long way down, before they intermingle. A forest of dead trees now met the view—fringed only on the river bank with living green. . . .

The approach was not without interest in a pecuniary point of view, but as a charming landscape one would not be thrown into ecstasies. The vast forest of dead timber looked in the distance more like a dark cloud that had, by some mischance approached too near the earth: for above it was the clear blue sky, and around it the emerald green of early spring. But stand up in the boat, for the tide is now high and you can see over the banks, and the whole aspect is changed. Beneath the dark setting is a carpet of lovely green; the young rice stimulated by the richness of the virgin soil was growing most luxuriantly, and would ere long hide from view the vast number of unsightly stumps.

But the trip was not quite over, two more miles up the Bull Creek had to be slowly made, for the current of this long river which flowed through the State and through North Carolina, where it was called the Yadkin and had its head-waters in Virginia, was very strong and the tide made but little impression, except to facilitate its downward progress. At length we reached the bachelor's retreat, that Eldorado of domestic felicity where I had lived in almost monastic seclusion, for it required only a small stretch of imagination to clothe the old moss covered live-oaks with their huge limbs sweeping to the ground, into the images of the past, particularly when we consider how many generations had passed away since they had been rooted into the ground, ere they had been awakened into—what shall I say? —life, or death, by the foot-fall of man.

To leave the boat, and walk through the remarkable trees was the work of a few moments, but to watch the countenance of their new mistress as she walked along was a study for some master, to have made for himself a name and given to the world a beautiful picture.

The little house was just as it had been left, nothing had disturbed its solitude, the wild turkey had taken his morning meal of acorns beneath the silent oaks, and the deer had shied away from the intrusive shanty and doubtless wondered by what title it had squatted on his possession. All was still and only the squirrel peeped at you when disturbed in his gambols through the thick branches. There was no porter's lodge, as there was no gate to be opened and no fences to keep intruders out. If the word "welcome" was not written on its portals, it was surely engrossed on the heart of him who turned the key and bade his visitors partake of its humble hospitality.

The huge mahogany side-board with its lion claws had not budged one inch; indeed it could not without treading on the out-spread feet of the oval dining table, which was not just then over-burdened with delicacies, but it gladly received the improvised repast. Well, we did not linger very long, nor did we visit the settlement a mile away on the other river, for the carriage and pair had not yet visited this secluded nook of God's creation. Nor will I record my father's many jokes at my expense to one who looked so inquisitively at all the surroundings. No one on the plantation ever knew of our coming or departure. . . .

We did not remain longer than six weeks on Waccamaw. Dinner and evening parties were the order of the day. We went to a very large evening party at Colonel J. J. Ward's at Brookgreen, the birthplace, by the way, of Washington Allston. Ward's daughter had recently been married to Dr. Flagg, and a large number of guests from the surrounding rivers were invited.[1] I will here say, that visiting in boats was necessary for all who lived on Sandy Island, on the West side of the Waccamaw, the Heriots, Belins, Petigrus, LaBruces, Vaux, etc., and those on the Peedee and Black rivers; some of the Allstons, Izards, Poinsetts (Joel R. Poinsett, Secretary of War, married the Widow Pringle, the mother of Julius Pringle who died in Rome), Reads, some of the Westons, Fords, etc. The party was kept up till the "wee sma' hours," and there was one who greatly enjoyed a regular old fashioned country dance to the music of sundry country fiddles. Worn out with the incidents of the evening, introductions to

---

[1] This is Mrs. Arthur B. Flagg, who, with her husband and children was drowned in the storm of 1893 which swept over Magnolia Beach. Allston, *Brookgreen,* p. 27.

so many new people, and dancing, she no sooner got into the carriage than she went to sleep and did not awake till we reached home.

John Ashe Alston, whose plantation was Strawberry Hill below Georgetown on the Waccamaw side of the river, gave me a large dinner party, only gentlemen present. He and I were great friends. He was the son of my Uncle William. He married Fanny Frasier.[2] . . . He and Dr. B. Burgh Smith, my uncle, were great friends and would frequently go to Strawberry Hill in the summer to look at the rice-crop. And when I would return, after a hard day's work, I would joke them about what they had seen and done during the day, and would find out, just what I suspected, that they had gone no further than the barn-yard and sat under the "winnowing house" in the shade eating watermelons. (A winnowing house is about 16 ft. square, built on high posts of 12 to 15 ft. The rice, after being threshed, is by high steps taken up and winnowed down through an aperture in the floor. . . .) "Yes," said John A., "I sent for my head man, Cuffee, and he said the crop was 'right poorly—that what with the dry-drought and the wet drought he 'spected the crop would be cut off right smart.' " Of course Cuffee's opinion was conclusive with his indulgent master, and as there was no use to 'cry over spilled milk' the only alternative, just then, was to have the true and faithful Cuffee order some fine, cool melons for his master's refreshment. . . . John Alston moved to Charleston, having purchased a very desirable home on Tradd Street on the west side of Charleston. He was a man of fine taste, fond of art and of refined society. His fine temper and social disposition made him very popular in the old city, and I look back with great pleasure to our long friendship, particularly when we lived on Debordieu and would go to the Club together. He was very fond of my father, and the latter of him. Our tastes were not the same in all things; field sports he never indulged in. Fine paintings were a delight to him; and he painted some creditable pictures and was very fond of talking of his Uncle Washington Allston, his mother's brother.[3] It was he who got up the Frasier Collection in Charleston. Charles Frasier of Charleston was a celebrated miniature painter. I remember him quite well; he lived on King Street and, in going to school, I frequently met him walking, with a little Scotch

[2] Mr. Alston uses this spelling of Fraser consistently.
[3] See genealogical table.

terrier following him. John A. induced all who had miniatures by Frasier to loan them for the exhibition. . . .

John A. was not much of a planter, as it is easy to discover, but it was the profession of the whole family, and as it had existed from generation to generation, he had to accept the situation. As I have said, he and my father were very fond of each other and they both had a fancy for politics—the latter to quite a great degree and the former in rather a mild form. Both went to the legislature for years, my father to the Senate and his nephew to the lower house.

[On one occasion] they were riding together on their way to Socastee which was high up the river out of the rice region. Their constituents were small farmers and men who made a living by cutting timber, hoops, poles, staves, shingles, etc. They were on their way to meet these people and John A. was to deliver the 4th of July oration, kiss the babies, praise the men, and compliment the women, etc. To neglect these duties would be to forfeit all respect and ruin all chances of preferment as a statesman. As they jogged on together, John A. said to his coachman, "Will." "Sir," was the ready and respectful reply. (Now Will was a huge black fellow, who would have been conspicuous in any crowd.) "You know, Will, I am going to make a 4th of July speech to-day." "Yes, Sir, I judge so, from what you and Marse Pinckney been talking about." "Now, Will, listen to me." (Will had been a close listener all the time and had enjoyed, without a change in his countenance, the many jests and pleasantries between uncle and nephew.) "You know there is much talk of mad dogs in the country—well, when I begin my speech, do you keep your eyes on me; never take them off, and if you see me halt, you yell out 'mad dog.' In the confusion I will take from my pocket, my written speech and so refresh my memory." Among these people, one who had to read his speech was totally unfit to represent them in Columbia.

He moved, as I have said, to Charleston, and when yellow fever broke out in the summer of 1856 (I think) he removed to Sullivan's Island, near the City, but unfortunately contracted the disease and died. He was in the very hey-day of life, of health, of happiness. I was then on Pawley's Island, and I hastened to my uncle William who was living on Debordieu. I will never forget his grief at the loss of this son—the only one who had been spared to his old age;

[4] Smith and Smith, *Charles Fraser,* make no reference to this exhibition.

. . . for he had lost his wife, whom he loved devotedly, and who was, as I have said, the sister of Washington Allston; all of his sons, five in number; and two daughters; only his twin daughters, Anna and Charlotte are now alive. (Charlotte died in 1896, Anna still lives at Rose Hill *alone;* the negroes who formerly belonged to the family are still devoted in their attention.)

His residence on Waccamaw, Rose Hill, had an air of culture and refinement. From the house to the rice fields a beautiful garden filled with shrubs and flowers gently sloped towards the river. He was one of the kindest and most indulgent masters I ever knew, and during the fierce civil war, and long years after, his large number of negroes were true and devoted to the family—indeed his daughters had no protectors but their servants, and I could write of many incidents of their love and fidelity, which would make the abolitionists of Boston green with jealousy. . . .

I have not mentioned how distressed I was on my return home under such happy circumstances, on being informed by my father that my favourite and much valued servant had been cruelly murdered at Woodbourne. This unhappy event occurred during my short absence and cast a dark shadow over the bright surroundings. It was not the money value which distressed me so greatly, for money could not have bought him nor replaced his devotion to me. William, or Cudjo as some called him, was of "royal descent." His father, whom I remember quite well, was a tall and handsome negro who had been a prince in his own country, was taken prisoner by some hostile tribe and sold into slavery and was bought by my grandfather with a number of others from a slave-ship, owned in Boston, which had brought its cargo to Charleston for sale. Caija, as I have said, was a wonderfully fine looking man and I quite remember how reticent and dignified he was. His son, Cudjo (which was, I fancy, a corruption of "Caija" or "Kaija," which is not so far away from "Kaiser") was given to me by my father. He was my head-man and trusted servant, and I feel sure I never said any unkind word to him. Indeed he looked upon my property as belonging to him, and I think it was on this account that he was killed. I had bought some eighty negroes recently, and one of them concealed himself behind a large tree and struck William over the head, from the effects of which he died. Had I been at home, it never would have occurred, and if it had I feel sure I could have saved him by prompt medical advice. As it was, the careless and ignorant over-seer thought he had been only slightly injured. A post-mortem showed a fracture.

His murderer escaped, but after a while I caught him myself and delivered him to the State authorities, who had failed to capture him. I gave a lawyer of high standing $150 to defend him and in so doing I occupied a very anomalous position—for on giving him his fee, I told him I was most anxious to have the man hung and begged him to request the judge, if such was to be his fate, to let the execution be on the spot where the murder occurred. I was summoned as a witness at the trial, and I merely allude to these facts to show you in what a singular position a *master* was sometimes placed. I wished the man hung and yet, as his owner, I felt bound to protect him; on the witness stand I could have turned the scales against the culprit by the strong circumstantial evidence in my possession, but I could not resist his imploring look. The man belonged to me. I had paid $1200 for him which I would gladly have lost to see him meet the full measure of the law, but I could not resist his appealing look for mercy at the hands of his master. My only testimony was that "I had been absent from the State at the time of William's death." . . . The man was severely punished by flogging and imprisonment and sold by the authorities out of the State. I lost in money one half of what I had paid for him, besides the lawyer's fees, etc., and what was of far more consideration, a servant, who was above all monied consideration, a valued and trusted friend. . . .

He [my father] gave me one of his best negroes to take, as far as he could, the place of the one I had lost and sent me his under overseer to replace the one I had turned off. Sam Kirton was one of the best men of his class I ever knew. When he came to me he was young and inexperienced and I only paid him $250 per annum. I increased his salary each year till he received $600 and then hearing that Pyatt of Georgetown would pay $1,000 for a good man, I recommended Kirton to him. I had to make him leave me, though I regretted his so doing. He saved money and when the war broke out went into the Confederate army and afterwards was employed by my uncle Charles Alston, who told me he was the best overseer he ever knew. His health failing, he bought a farm on the Coosa river, near Rome, and when I was there in 1880 he came to see me, a married man and comfortably off. Of course there were brutal overseers but they were the exceptions; and Mrs. Stowe's New England overseer with a

Southern name was one. I never employed any but humane men. To say the least, self interest dictated this course. . . .

Of course I made frequent visits to Woodbourne. I would gallop there, and then back, or drive my bob-tailed greys, but I sadly missed the hearty welcome from my trusted and much appreciated servant who had been so cruelly murdered. It was long before I took my accustomed and necessary interest in the heavy work before me, and so interfered with by the loss I had sustained.

The society of Wacamaw was refined and cultivated. My uncle, Charles Alston, and his family lived at Fairfield; his wife, my Aunt Emma, was a daughter of John Julius Pringle, once Attorney General of the United States.[5] She was a very handsome woman, and I have heard that La Fayette remarked that she and Mrs. Longstreet, the sister of your great-grandmother Fitzsimons, were the handsomest women he had seen in America. I heard this from my father. Then, there was John Izard Middleton and his family, He was a son of Henry Middleton, Minister to Russia; his wife, my Cousin "Sally," was a daughter of my uncle John Ashe Alston. She was very lovely in appearance and in character. Mr. Middleton lived at Crowfield, named after the Middleton estate in England. When owned by my uncle John it was know as Bannockburn. . . . Next to Weehawka was Hagley, the former home of Governor Joseph Alston and his wife Theodosia. . . . The Oaks and Hagley belonged to my uncle Joseph. At the time I am writing of, Hagley belonged to Plowden Weston. He was an only son of Francis Marion Weston; his mother was a cousin by [the] same name, whom he married in England. Plowden Weston owned Hagley, and he was married to Miss Emily, daughter of Sir Edward Esdell of England.

Plowden Weston and myself were life long friends, and I remember calling upon his wife, then a bride, about a month before my marriage. She was an intelligent woman and had a wonderfully fine voice. When we lived at Woodbourne she would come to see us frequently and spend several days with us. Of course she called at once at True Blue and that first visit ripened into a life-long friendship. She died in London, some years ago. Hagley had a very large and commodious house, and two large rooms, communicating, were filled with choice and elegantly bound books. This library was worth at the present

[5] Although appointed Attorney-General of the United States, John Julius Pringle declined the office. See *Dictionary of American Biography,* XV, 238.

day some $50,000 or over. It was all lost during the war. Plowden Weston was educated at Cambridge, England. He was a very indulgent master, and had the interest on nearly, if not quite, $1,000,000 to live on. I think I have mentioned that he went into the Confederate army, and died from exposure. . . .

The South was ever a book-reading, but *not* a book-writing people, and thus so many facts of deep interest are unrecorded, and come down to future generations in the shape of tradition; whereas, at the North every minute occurrence is jotted down, revised, and corrected according to circumstances. . . .

Some few war histories have been written at the South, but thus far only writers of negro stories, with few exceptions, have been found acceptable to northern readers. We had as gifted men at the South, as the North could boast of, but strange to say their taste did not lie in book-making. I remember so well when William Gilmore Simms first began to write his romances and historical novels how little encouragement he received at the South. Indeed he was rather looked down upon. Of course, I do not pretend to compare Simms to Scott, but I do say, that Sir Walter Scott never gave to Scottish life a better, and more truthful photograph than did Simms [to South Carolina] of the period just before and during the war of the revolution. The people, their manner of life, and the description of the country is beautifully portrayed, and they who love to wander back into the past, cannot fail to be grateful to William Gilmore Simms. (Simms made the great mistake of writing too rapidly.) I remember Governor Hammond of South Carolina saying to me that it was "strange that people did not set more store on Simms." That he "looked upon him as a wonderfully fine writer."[6] And James H. Hammond was, at least, a gifted man, as his records as Senator in Congress proved.

Yet Simms died a poor man. I remember him so well, when I lived in Columbia, where so many congregated from all parts of the South. He portrayed very vividly, and I think quite truthfully, the characteristics of the North American Indian. As a writer he does not rank, on the whole, with Cooper, but all must admit that the latter's portrayal of Indian character was a complete failure, as far

[6] On the relationship of Hammond and Simms see Oliphant, Odell, and Eaves (eds.), *The Letters of William Gilmore Simms*, Vol. I (Columbia, 1952), p. lvi.

as truthfulness goes.[7] Of course his sea tales are good, and the *Two Admirals* wonderfully so. It is a great pity that the American Indian should have been well nigh exterminated, if he possessed the noble instincts which Cooper credits him with. Of course, Simms weaves much romance around his tales of the Revolution, but there is no book, or set of books, which will give one a better, or more truthful account of the times therein described. Always remember that the Carolinas were completely under British domination. John Rutledge, Governor and Dictator, had no abiding place, but had to follow the little band of patriots who were concealed in the dense swamps of the low country. Surely there was something more than romantic, even if severely truthful, in the lives of Marion, Sumter, Horry, etc., and the men who followed them from a pure unadulterated love of Country.

Is it not wonderfully strange that with such resources, Simms was the only novelist in Carolina, who undertook to paint in glowing colors scenes which should be almost sacred to the youthful southern heart. His description of life in Charleston when occupied by the British is very interesting and very real. Many of the old houses described by him are still standing. . . .

Well, our sojourn on Waccamaw for the present season was over, and we returned to Charleston where we spent some little while at the Charleston Hotel on Meeting Street. . . .

We passed part of the summer at my father's mountain home, sometimes spending a week or two in Clarksville. In the fall we took Mrs. Fitzsimons and her two little girls with us in our carriage to Columbia, S.C.

. . . I remember so well we met a circus in full blast and much to the amusement of our party I called a halt and witnessed the performance. We were on our way to make the Hamptons a visit, by invitation. We traveled in my carriage with the bob-tailed grays and my grey trotting pony by way of a change for me. This was the finest pony for this purpose I ever owned. He would never move under fire, and would remain just where I left him. My father and

[7] Mark Twain fully sustains Mr. Alston's estimate of Cooper as an authority on Indian life in his essay "Fenimore Cooper's Literary Offenses," republished in E. B. and K. S. White, *A Subtreasury of American Humor* (New York, 1941), pp. 519-30.

self would shoot together and he was far the best shot, but when I out-numbered him he would always give the little grey the credit. Nothing would excite the animal. I have fired both barrels, while resting on my saddle, so as not to prepare him by lifting up my gun, while he was drinking from a road-side rivulet and I could feel the water gurgle in his throat with the same regularity.

I would sometimes buy a number of Indian ponies in Habersham and Rabun Counties, and send them to the low country in the fall. I would sell those I did not want, and so reduce the price of those I kept, to less than nothing. I had ever a great passion for horses. . . . In Columbia I sent my carriage and horses to Waccamaw, as we had struck the railroad, and from there we would go on to Charleston by rail and to Waccamaw by boat. . . .

A half century ago traveling was very far behind what it is now. No palace cars with so many luxuries attached, where one could rest and sleep in comfort, rather than to sit bold upright and nod in a car where all sorts and conditions of people were crowded together. On looking backward the only wonder is how we could bear, so amiably, all the hardships of railroad travel. It is true one made a little better time than the deserted stage coach, but the latter was more comfortable and sociable and far less dangerous to life and limb; and you at least escaped being now and then pierced through and through by a "snake head" as the flat iron was called, when it became detached from the wooden sleeper on which it was nailed, and poked through the bottom of the car and pinned some luckless passenger through his vitals to the top of the coach. On the other hand, there was less rush in those primitive days of railroad travel, and the stops more frequent and of longer duration, the sociability of the old stage coach not having been eradicated from the traveler by steam. When the whistle blew and the conductor called out "all aboard," he would politely see that all *were* aboard, and if not, would wait a reasonable time for stragglers. . . .

I have seen the engineer and train hands when not pushed for time, stop to gather a few tempting blackberries by the roadside, and on one occasion, a lady whose name and family were highly respected, and who was traveling from the sea-board to the mountains and who had the misfortune to lose one of her nine cats, which was overcome by the heat and want of home comforts and conveniences, had the train stopped that her pet could be buried. Poor Pussy was wrapped in a fair white cloth and laid gently in a basket and taken by her sad mistress, followed by the family, and some of the more sympathetic or curious passengers and gently laid away by one of the train hands, after he had scraped out a hole beneath some majestic pine. Poor Puss, her nine lives had been suddenly cut short, a victim to early railroad traveling.

But I am "off the track," a common occurrence in the days I write of, and I must retrace my steps. . . .

In Columbia we stayed with young Wade Hampton (the present General) and his wife, who was Miss Margaret Preston of Virginia, sister of William C. and John S. Preston, both men of note in Carolina. Mrs. Hampton, Margaret Preston, was a most charming woman, very handsome and very lovely. The rest of the family went to Millwood, where Colonel Wade Hampton and his daughter lived, about five miles from the City. Millwood was then a beautiful country residence where refinement dwelt and hospitality loved to linger. Colonel Hampton was an eminently handsome man; his wife, who had long been dead was Ann Fitzsimons, the sister of Colonel Paul Fitzsimons. He and Colonel H. were devoted friends. We passed a week or ten days at Millwood, little dreaming that in ten years I would reside in Columbia, and be a frequent visitor at Millwood. Colonel Hampton, at this time, owned the finest racing stable in Carolina. . . . Monarch and Sovereign were among his noted horses. Both of these horses were bred at Hampton Court. Colonel Hampton was most liberal, and I have understood that he often presented a thorough-bred colt to some of his guests who greatly admired the same. He more than once had them led out for me to see, and though I was passionately fond of horses, I fear the Colonel thought me very unappreciative. His father, General Wade Hampton, Senior, resided during his lifetime at Woodlands, some two miles nearer to the river. He was very conspicuous during the wars of the long ago and amassed a very large fortune. He was married three or four times and was, I have understood, a man of an ungovernable temper, and many marvelous stories are told of him.[8]

We fully enjoyed our visit, for they are a most charming family, [spent] a week or so in Charleston, and then [went] off by sea for old Waccamaw.

---

[8] There are sketches of the first and third Wade Hamptons, with references to the second, in the *Dictionary of American Biography,* VII, 212-15.

The "Nina" . . . plied between the City and plantations on the Waccamaw river, and was a great convenience to the planters. Fort Sumter did not then command the entrance to the harbour; a few rocks, which from time to time had been dumped thereon by vessels of the General Government, were to form in time a foundation for the fort, [but now] only showed themselves above the mudflats between the North and South Channels. . . . On this same flat the British ship "Acteon" grounded on the 28th June 1776, and was burned to prevent her falling into the hands of the victorious Americans. And so this old harbour is ever memorable as having been the scene of three heroic conflicts, the fierce fight between the Carolinians and the pirates in the year 1718, the gallant defense of Fort Moultrie during what the British call the Rebellion of 1776, and the more than heroic defense of Fort Sumter in the War between the States.[9] . . .

The "Nina" left at 7 A.M. and on a beautiful November morning I stood on the upper deck with one so dear beside me, where I could point out so many objects of interest. [We departed] from the wharf at the foot of Tradd Street, near where the residence of Charles Pinckney (the father of General Charles Cotesworth and Thomas Pinckney) stands; for in those colonial days all this portion of the city of Charleston was a water front, not the busy Bay Street of the present day. We steamed out into the harbour: Castle Pinckney was left behind, and the "Battery" with its long sea-wall extending along the Cooper and around to the Ashley river; the handsome residences, live oaks and green sward freshened and lit up by the early morning sun; the calm blue water of the expansive harbour, with the group of tall pines on James Island to the right, and Haddrell's point to the left. The City receding in the distance, in the midst of which looms up the tall spire of old St. Michael's was always a lovely picture to me, so dearly associated with all my early memories. As Georgetown is 100 miles to the north we steam through the North Channel. That pile of rock and stone to the right is where Fort Sumter now stands. Cargoes have been dumped on this mud flat, and now the water is rippling over them at high tide. To the left, so near, that you can almost throw a biscuit on the beach, is Sullivan's Island, the summer re-

[9] These attacks on Charleston harbor are described in Wallace, *South Carolina: A Short History,* pp. 94, 285, 539 ff.

sort of Charlestonians and visitors from the interior, who seek the sea breezes of the Atlantic. The numberless cottages you see belong to persons in the City, that large Hotel is the Moultrie House, and the Fort is Fort Moultrie, named after General Moultrie by General Rutledge after his gallant defense of Fort Sullivan, which was the name it bore on the 28th June, 1776.[10] It was then built of Palmetto logs but is now somewhat modernized, and it was from here that Anderson shifted his quarters to Fort Sumter during the night in 1861.

Whilst we are in a stone's throw of Fort Moultrie, where as a little boy I used to paddle in the water and catch crabs in the little ponds on the beach left by the receding tide, I must tell you of a little incident which befell me here some few years before the late war. I was living for the time being on the Sand Hills near Augusta. In September I came to Charleston, on my way to Waccamaw, and as the "Nina" did not leave till the next morning, I went over to Sullivan's Island to see my Aunt Lizzie, Mrs. Arthur P. Hayne, who had a cottage for the summer close to the beach. I met on the ferry boat many Charleston friends, and I remarked that "we were going to have a storm." As there was no apparent reason to them for such a prophecy they laughed at my prognostication.

I found my Aunt's house pretty full, but as I was ever at home with her, I slept on a lounge in the parlour. About mid-night I looked out, the wind had freshened up, and it was black and stormy. . . . By morning all communication with the City was cut off, and by noon we found ourselves in the midst of a fierce gale, and the ladies were terribly alarmed. Colonel Hayne was then an old man and the fire that had been instilled into him by General Jackson during the Creek War and battle at New Orleans, where he was one of Jackson's aides,[11] had begun slowly to burn out—besides, he knew very little of hurricanes on the Carolina coast, where I had been cradled and had learned by a sort of instinct to discern the signs of a coming hurricane. My aunt and her guests would not consent to remain in the cottage so close to the beach and built on the sand which would melt away should the water reach it; so all determined to seek protection in Fort Moultrie. The old Colonel gave his consent reluctantly, but was too polite to object.

[10] *Ibid.*, p. 294.
[11] *Ibid.*, p. 371.

The rain was falling and the wind blew fiercely, and how to move the ladies and a little infant only a few weeks old was a problem, for it was most difficult to keep one's feet during the march. . . . On reaching the Fort, we found people crowding in. This was several years before the war, but there was at the time some unpleasantness between Carolina and the General Government, and on [our] appearing at the entrance, the officer in command laughingly "twitted" me on taking protection under the flag of the United States. I had never intended to remain in a crowded Fort when I had the selection of so many downy beds at the cottage, so I politely told him that I preferred to stand one big squall on the outside of the cottage, rather than so many minor ones inside the Fort.

I soon regained the deserted house—the family in ignorance of my intention; fastened down the windows, secured the doors, chose the most luxurious bed, and was soon wrapped in a profound slumber. Hearing a tremendous pounding at the door I jumped up, found it was near breakfast time, and the family and servants clamoring for admittance, which was only postponed till I could make a respectable appearance. I found that the water during the night had risen half-way under the house, but had receded before doing any damage. The morning was clear and I had to hurry up to catch the boat for the city, and the "Nina" for Waccamaw. My friends on the former were quite amazed at the fulfillment of prophesy.

But these were days before the signal service; electricity was then very cloudy and had not been taught to say "good-morning" or "good-night" to mankind through the telephone, but was only recognized as a striking enemy. Science has knocked the nose of superstition out of joint; though I confess, that in my nature, have been engrafted certain signs which will not down at its bidding. The monotonous lowing of a cow, the whisking around of a pig with a whisp of straw in its mouth, the hoarse cry of the rain-crow, etc., give signs which are not to be unheeded. But far more unerring and delightful than all is the sweet note of the little swamp thrush: when the rain has been pouring down all night and the out-look in the morning is dismal in the extreme, you go to the window to ponder as to how you can pass the day, the woods around you reeking wet, the clouds above you too heavy to move: when, deep in the recesses of the swamp you hear the little thrush's cheerful note, then in nine times out of ten, the sullen clouds will begin to lift and patches of blue sky prepare the way for the sun's cheerful face. How do these little birds know so much—or, rather, how do we know so little? . . .

A long winter was before me, as I had never been so long absent from my work, and debts of over $40,000 were to be paid, year by year, more land to be cleared, and a dwelling to be built at Woodbourne so that by the following year our home would be established there. No time for field sports now, no St. Cecelia and Jockey Club balls. Woodbourne was seventeen miles from True Blue and much time was consumed on the road. And so I will not write of a happy winter of work out doors and pleasures within.

In March 1849 we left the rice-fields and moved to the Sand Hills near Augusta, and in June when the weather became hot we went to Ka-a, taking our darling little boy with us.

This was a very remarkable spring. On or about the middle of April we had a heavy fall of snow, which killed the crops of corn and cotton, etc., far and near. All had to be planted over. Here was the great advantage rice had all over other crops; just raise up the gates of the trunks and let on the water and so cover up the young rice, where neither wind nor frost could reach.

But this summer was a fearful one to me. My dearest Mary was taken violently ill with an inflammatory fever, which the mountain doctors, knowing that we had come from the low-country, mistook for malarial fever, and in consequence of which, very nearly proved fatal. For long weeks she lay between life and death, one of the four physicians who were in attendance coming from Athens, sixty miles away and no railroad. At length the mist of gloom began to lift, and the bright sun of hope to dispel the leaden clouds of dark despair and untold misery. . . .

And so the summer and fall had passed away and we returned to Waccamaw, and in a few weeks after to housekeeping at Woodbourne. The house having been finished [was] painted red with a slate coloured roof of seven gables, and twelve rooms, all built and painted by my man, Richmond.

I bought Richmond and his wife from my father for $1500 cash, and he proved himself faithful to the end, when I turned him over to the tender care of "Uncle Sam." He remained where I had left him, near Columbia, South Carolina, and the last time I saw him was in Charleston a few years after the war. He came down to see me, and one morning as I was dressing in the old yellow parlour of the King Street house, where I had passed the night, as I had so many during my childhood, I heard a knock at the door. Of course, I was very glad to see him, and on shaking hands with him I noticed he was not exactly in a "dude's" attire. I asked him to sit down till I had finished dressing, when suddenly, I turned to him and asked him if he had ever heard that I had left him and his wife—he had no children—free by my will. He said, "No," but seemed much affected and asked why I had not told him and was mortified on my telling him that I did not do so, for fear he would wish me dead. I will never forget his answer—"Ah, Master, I have never known freedom since you left me." Well, in his case, it was strictly true. He was my head carpenter and engineer when I planted rice, but when I moved to Columbia he was a far freer man than I was. He had nothing to do except what he chose, lived in a city, and was fed and clothed and doctor bills paid. . . .

And so Richmond built the Woodbourne house and was only assisted when he handled timbers too heavy for him. The lime was burned on the seashore (shell-lime) and the plastering was done by my father's plasterers, and thus it was of domestic manufacture, and set apart to domestic happiness. . . .

But I must get back to my out-door life. The axes are ringing through the dense swamp and glimpses of light is seen, as one by one the tall trees come crashing to the earth to make way, in time, for waving fields of green and gold. The work is slow and arduous, week by week, month by month, year by year. Failure is not to be dreamed of, too much is at stake. Through fire and water, through felling and burning the work goes on, and when the sun goes down, it alone brings rest. The river banks now are nearly four miles in length, and protect the land for the over-flowing tides, but this is a mere beginning, though a great luxury, in-as-much-as the hands can walk to their work and not come down in flats. But the winter has gone, and the land, already cleared, must be prepared for planting, the stubble of the previous crop burned off, and the land trenched for the coming crop. This work is much lighter now, for the virgin soil is not polluted with grass and forces the rice to grow with great rapidity. But, as I have said, the sun is sinking behind the dense forest, and it is nearly time to "knock off." . . .

Our home was comfortably furnished, but far from elaborately, no Brussels carpets, but all the solid comforts of life, which now began in earnest. It was hard to be reconciled to enforce such a life on one so young and so lovely, but if this was to be a business success, there was nothing else to do. A large amount of money was invested here before my marriage, and so it was either this or long months of separation. And so the house was built and furnished and occupied in one of the loneliest and most inaccessible places imaginable. This peninsula between two large rivers, uncleared swamps all around, the huge cypress hung in festoons of gray moss, which until the axe could clear them away obstructed all view of the river in front; a large impenetrable bay (Wolf's Bay) in the rear, where foxes and wild cats felt themselves safe from harm. (A "bay" in the low country of Carolina was a swampy area with a growth of low stunted bushes and tangled vines. As the soil was peaty and rested on a sand foundation it was worthless for cultivation.)

This then was not an enchanting spot, but here we lived, cut off from the world, and yet how fondly does memory retrace its weary care laden steps and bask once more in the sunshine of so many happy hours, where

"There is society where none intrudes." . . .

The candles have just been lighted and a bright and cheerful wood fire helps to shed its influence on the lovely picture before me, as I stand at the door and gaze upon it. A beautiful young mother, sweetly dressed is seated near, while at her feet, on the rug, her little boy is playing with the folds of her gown. I have been on the lake duck shooting and come in laden with beautiful green-head mallards and more beautiful wood-duck, and I draw the child away and surround him with the game and we clap our hands to see him try to embrace them all at once. Surely there was joy and untold happiness in that room which words could not describe, even though the tangled moss swayed to and fro from the gloomy cypress, and the huge horned owl, in melancholy tone, hooted to its mate across the river. The wild outlook was hidden from the happy hearts within, where cheerfulness smiled at all extreme gloom. . . .

Cut off as we were from the outer world, there were no passers-by; those who came to Woodbourne came to see us. From Waccamaw Neck there was no approach, as I have said, save by water. I had a road opened from my residence to Yahanee Ferry along the Bull Creek to give an outlet from the plantation to the road from Georgetown to Conwayboro, so that we might ride or drive for pleasure, and, also, to send for the mail, which was left for me at the ferry every other day. To miss the mail was a dire calamity. . . . Those who cared enough for us to make us visits, of course, had to be invited to remain to dinner or for the night. But our home was commodious and the barn-yard abundantly supplied with poultry, turkeys, geese, ducks, and chickens of various breeds, from the huge Shanghais to the delicate game fowl, and then the larder was also well filled with wild-duck, etc.

Two miles above Woodbourne on the Waccamaw there were large saw-mills from which were exported pine lumber of all kinds to the West Indies. These vessels would pass in front of my house, and I would frequently lay in all the fruit I wanted at a trifling cost.

The Reverend Alexander Glennie and his wife would come to us once every fortnight. He came always to dinner, after which he would teach the negro children their catechism and preach to all of my negroes at night. They always had a half holiday on these occasions, so as to let them brush up and make a respectable appearance. It was a law that all should attend. Of course the majority were only too anxious to do so, but there were some who preferred to hunt, fish, or sleep, and so I had to make the headmen call at each house and compel them to come in. I had a Church built conveniently, and my family, myself, and guests always attended. It was quite wonderful what retentive memories they [the negroes] had, for few could read. The minister would always read the evening services of the Episcopal Book of Common Prayer and always, too, the same Psalter so as to enable the congregation to respond, which they did most accurately and devoutly. But I do so well remember one evening when the Bishop (Davis) accompanied Mr. Glennie and was to preach that evening, and all were rigged out in their Sunday's best, when in the midst of the service, while all were standing, one of the men, full six feet in height, went fast asleep and fell over the benches, and all came down with a crash to the floor, to the amusement of the congregation and the mortification of the performer, whose specific gravity so greatly outweighed his spiritual zeal. The next day when I tried to lecture him and told him how deeply mortified I felt when I saw him measure his length on the floor, in the presence of the Bishop of the State, I could but laugh at his discomfiture and from that day I had the code revised and told my head man that he must no longer compel the negroes to attend service; that I would be glad to have them go to Church, but that I left it optional with them. . . .

To leave home, in these days I write of, was not a troublesome affair, for the house was committed to the care of those servants left behind, to be swept and aired as occasion required.

After a few days at True Blue we left for Charleston, and then for Augusta, en route for Ka-a. . . . A portion of my father's family were to occupy my Cottage by the Sea at the southern extremity of Pawley's Island, and as Ka-a was to be vacant we concluded to spend the summer there. My horses were sent ahead and met us at Athens, the then terminus of that branch of the Georgia railroad. Our trip from True Blue to Charleston was most lovely. On both sides of the river the young rice shaded the highly prepared soil in tints of luxuriant green while swaying to and fro on the tops of the slender shrubs which fringed the banks; little groups of gaily attired bob-o-links were cheerfully warbling forth their notes of thanks for what these rice fields had given to them, ere they departed to levy on the wheat fields farther north. . . . But we must not linger longer for the "Nina" is nearly ready to start out into Winyah Bay. . . . But as we gaze over the vast expanse, and are so rapidly steaming along in spite of wind or wave, how forcibly am I reminded of my experience not very many years before.

I had left old Debordieu in July to make a trip North and so take in Saratoga, Newport, and New York. I boarded a little schooner on the Waccamaw, on a steaming hot day in July. The vessel was bound for Charleston and carried a load of rice below, and innumerable coops of chickens and young ducks on deck for the planters who lived in the city during the summer. There was hardly air enough to reach the bar, but with the help of an ebb tide, we managed to float to the ocean, where a dead calm over-took us. . . . The sun poured down his red hot rays with intense fury which was mirrored on the glassy surface of the ocean, and it took the aid of *two* umbrellas to save your complexion and prevent the skin from peeling off, and so ruin a fellow for his debut at Saratoga; one to shield you from the vertical rays and the other from the reflection on the liquid surface below. These was no escape to the cabin, for that consisted of a wee bit of an aperture below with two bunks, one for the captain and the other for any distinguished guest. . . . Suffice it to say that . . . our next [day] was a counterpart of the one I have tried to paint so truthfully. Sometimes the sailors would get aboard the yawl and with a rope fastened to the vessel tow her where some current of air might perchance strike her—but all in vain. I am glad, however, to say that during the second night I heard the "yo-he-ho" of the sailors and felt the motion of the becalmed schooner, and by ten o'clock the following day the tall white spire of old St. Michael's brought peace to one troubled soul. To go to my uncle Charles Alston's house on the Battery, and to plunge into a glorious bath, and to sit down to a home dinner of okra soup first, and a bottle of old Madeira last, fully compensated for reading in the next morning's *Courier* among the list of arrivals "Pr. Schooner *Peru* Capt. Cope—three days from Georgetown, S.C. laden with bbls. of rice &c. J M Alston, Passenger."

. . .

I have given thus far a picture of a planter's life in the low country of Carolina, and so I will not dwell much more on our life at Woodbourne, as it is becoming monotonous to anyone who should read these pages—so was it eminently so to me, to endure and enforce such an extremely lonely life on one so dear to me, and the little group which had gathered about our knees.

I was making headway in my business and could not well trust the same into the hands of agents. In order to render matters pleasanter, and yet not to sacrifice, in any way, my planting interests, I purchased from my friend, Plowden Weston, one hundred acres of land on the sea shore of Waccamaw. It was a beautifully wooded tract of land, live and water oaks, magnolias, and cedars, etc., on a bold salt-water creek, near Murrell's Inlet, so named from the pirate who was said to have buried treasures in that neighborhood. Here I built an eight room residence. The plan I drew myself, and the work was done by Richmond, to whom I have alluded. The frame was all finished at Woodbourne, moved across the river in flats and hauled to the sea shore by ox teams. Richmond did the whole work—of course with the assistance of some of my men to lift the heavy timbers, etc. The planters spent money freely, yet they lived as much as possible within themselves. All that could be done at home was done. Of course, all the fine work, such as doors, windows, panneling, plastering, painting, etc., was not domestic. I hired a New York builder to put up an oval stair way, as this feature in the Woodbourne residence was not particularly artistic. Altogether the Sunnyside style of architecture was quite an improvement on that of Woodbourne. But as Rome was, they say, not built in a day, so it consumed a winter and summer and a month or two over, to have our new home completed. Cut off as we had been at Woodbourne from all society except such as came prepared to remain with us for the day or longer, we could now visit and receive visitors and drive to the All Saints Parish Church, or to St. John's, which was only a short distance from Sunnyside. I owned a pew at the Parish Church, which was of brick, and where many of the family are buried, my Aunt Mary Rutledge Smith, and my dear Grandmother Smith, John Ashe Alston and others. St. John's had been but recently built and there I owned two pews.

Although surrounded by woods I had grates put in some of the rooms in which coal was burned so as to give an air of city life. We were two miles from Woodbourne, and every day I could look after my planting interest and return to dinner. My table was most bountifully supplied; the plantation contributed all the poultry, etc., and the deep creek in front of the house all the fish, oysters, clams, crabs, shrimp, etc., to say nothing of the game from both places. The salt marshes here and opposite Debordieu, some fifteen miles below, were much wider than those between these two points, and could only be forded at low tide. . . .

I was quite in love with our new home; that feeling of isolation which was ever attended with so great responsibility was now removed, for here we were within reach of medical aid should such be needed. In this particular we were much blessed at Woodbourne, for I do not remember having to send for a physician whilst we resided there for any of the family save myself, when I had contracted a severe illness from having slept in damp sheets whilst in Charleston. And so we resided at our new home always till the first of July when we would seek a cooler atmosphere, either in the mountains or on Pawley's Island, some twelve miles below, where we could enjoy the uninterrupted breeze of the ocean and the society of all who passed the summer there. In October we would return to Sunnyside.

Sometimes in the winter we would take the steamer for Charleston and spend a month at the Mills House or Charleston Hotel.

But I will not dwell any longer on our residence on Waccamaw. Our children were fast growing old enough to need the advantages of schools, and so I quietly determined to sell Woodbourne as soon as I could obtain that which I considered its value. My neighbor, Henry Buck, had made me sundry offers for the property which I had refused. One day whilst I felt that it would be wise to sell I rode to Laurel Hill, the residence of Francis Marion Weston, where I usually had my rice pounded for the Charleston market and went to the mill and said to Tom Daggett, the miller, "How would you like to make some hundreds of dollars between this and breakfast?" I then told him to go as soon as he closed the mill and offer Woodbourne to Henry Buck for $50,000. I remarked to him, that if he found him in the humor to make the purchase, he could take $45,000. And so the place on which I had expended so much time, labor, and money, passed out of my hands before they had retired for the night. Nothing was said of the transaction till the papers were signed. I had lived so long away from the world that I did not wish any one to know that I even contemplated selling, for I was both pleased and distressed—pleased that I now had it in my power to reward my dear Mary for the long years of patient endurance, and grieved at seeing the home of our early married life pass into the hands of strangers. I did not even tell *her* of the sale till there was nothing left but to accept that which I deemed was the best, and now I had nothing to do, for I had hired all of my negroes to the new owner of Woodbourne. . . .

So, as there was no inducement to live at Sunnyside which was only an adjunct to my rice plantation, I therefore sold the latter place to my brother Charles and took in payment so many negroes which my father had given to him. I had previously sold to Charles a portion of the rice land belonging to the Woodbourne tract, which adjoined some land which had been given to him by my father, and for which he had given me his bond and notes. This was never paid. The war came on in less than three years, and Charles died soon after its close, insolvent, and rice lands depreciated to less than one fourth their former value, till at the time at which I am now writing, the best equipped plantations can be leased or rented for the small amount of taxes for which they are assessed. . . .

The amount due me by my brother Charles, principal and interest, when the war closed was very nearly $20,000, for which I received nothing. Such is war—and this could have been avoided had the politicians on both sides seen fit to have done so. I did not give up residing at Sunnyside for a year after I had sold Woodbourne.

My movements in all business transactions were always rapid, so as soon as I had found a purchaser for Sunnyside I boarded a steamer, went to Charleston, and took the railroad for Columbia. I reached Columbia that night. At breakfast at the hotel I looked over the morning paper and selected from the list of residences offered for sale one that I thought best of, walked out, and took a bird's eye view of it, called on the agent, asked the price, which my utter indifference brought down to the lowest cash figure. I then inspected the property minutely and called on Colonel Hampton (now General) and told him I would write him, if on my return home his cousin [Mrs. Alston] . . . was pleased with the purchase, and [I would] ask of him to close the trade; and [that] when the titles were ready, I would send him a sight draft for the whole amount—$6,000. The lot was a very large one, beautifully ornamented with trees and hedges and the house, a brick one, built in antique style, though by no means an old one.

Of course, there was a vast deal to be done, and so in less than a week I was back at Sunnyside; and, after consulting my dear Mary, I wrote Colonel Hampton and commenced to prepare for the move. In a week or two I returned to Columbia and took possession of the new purchase, engaged mechanics and painters and put it in order, returned to Charleston, and laid out $2,000 in furniture, carpets, curtains, etc., and returned for the last time to dear old Waccamaw. I had sold my negroes to Governor John L. Manning of South Carolina, except about thirty-five who had been in the family all their lives. These, with the exception of my house servants I hired out to the railroad near Columbia, where I could look after them. They seemed perfectly contented with their new life, but I received only a small compensation, as I had to pay all of their doctor's bills, taxes, etc.

We soon had our household goods packed and shipped and then bade a final adieu to the home of my fathers. I will not pretend to write of those memories which cluster around me. The belief that

I would visit again the land where I had lived so long and the people among whom so many long years had been passed relieved, in some degree, the pain which pressed upon me, as I would involuntarily lift my hat to the old familiar homes I was passing, as we steamed down the river. But I had looked upon them all for the last time, for in less than three years, ere we had been well fixed in our new home, the fatal civil war broke over the South, and so cut off all hope of such fond anticipation; and thus the home of my childhood and of my early married life had faded from my sight forever. Thank God, I left it in all its peaceful beauty, when the wild flowers which clustered on either bank, breathed only of that tranquility which will ne'er come again. . . .

Our new home in Columbia, South Carolina, was a lovely one, where peace and plenty dwelt and where I fondly hoped we would pass the rest of our days. The people who resided here were proverbial for their refinement and hospitality, and our reception among them was in keeping with the same. In a short time we felt that we were surrounded by the best and truest of friends. . . .

I had accomplished what I had worked for, had paid off a heavy debt of $45,000 and had about $135,000 in what was then considered the very best investments in South Carolina. I now fondly hoped that I could rest, as I did not owe one dollar and sadly needed some let up from the strain I had endured for so many years. . . .

Peace reigned over the country, and never was the South more prosperous than at the period between 1848 and 1860. . . .

5

The War Years and After

HOW CAN one refrain from touching on politics when so much suffering followed in the wake of the Civil War? . . . I remember so well having . . . met several distinguished members of the Convention [Democratic convention of 1860] —General Preston of Kentucky, Mr. August Belmont of New York, and several others. Mr. Belmont could not conceal his disappointment at Stephen Douglas' not being nominated. Had this been, the war would have been averted for the time being at least. . . . It was wholly our fault that Lincoln was elected, and the Republican party put in power. The Charleston convention failed to nominate, and the Baltimore convention a little later put out three candidates. Surely common sense should have foretold what the issue would be, and so having invited defeat we should have abided by our folly and quietly awaited the course of the new party in power. Under the Constitution we could have secured our rights—the rights of those States which first formed the Union—the original thirteen which formed a union for mutual protection, but certainly with no agreement to yield the rights of the individual States. But no, we plunged into war, a cruel civil war which of all others should have been carefully weighed, and avoided if possible. . . .

For Carolina to secede from the Union, not knowing if any of her sister states would unite with her, . . . was a desperate alternative; and the only solution, apart from feeling that the compact which bound her to the Union had been broken, is the fact that the Carolinians had ever been a self-reliant people. In the earliest days of the English settlements in America, Jamestown, Plymouth and Charleston, in the order here given, the colony of the latter being so widely separated from the others, had to rely solely on themselves. Between Jamestown and Charleston, [with] several hundreds of miles of forest and only an Indian trail between, threatened by the Spaniards from below, the Indians in the rear and pirates by sea, the Carolinians were taught to look for no outside help. This spirit, I presume, was what animated them to cut loose from the bond which they more than once chafed under. . . .

Some of the ablest men of the North, thoroughly versed in constitutional history always contended that no state of the original thirteen should be coerced to remain in the Union when the majority of its people deemed themselves oppressed by the general government. Had South Carolina been permitted to secede peaceably I question if any of her sister states would have joined her. She in time would have returned to the fold, all difficulties settled and a fearful civil war averted. . . .

But the struggle is about to begin. The Ordinance of Secession has been passed amid a silence as profound as it was painful to many who were assembled to witness a ceremony fraught with so much uncertainty. The gallant little state was now divorced from her marriage ties. Was the cause sufficient that such an extreme step be taken? . . .

On a visit to Charleston I was at the Mills House when the "Star of the West" was fired on and beaten off by the Confederates. Crowds went to the Battery. On my return I met Mr. James L. Petigru, a life-long Union man.[1] He put his arm in mine as we walked on together and on my asking him "How all this would end?" he said, "Alston, don't you know that the whole world is against slavery? So, if the South is to fight for that, rest assured it is lost, never mind which side wins," and he was right. . . .

That the word *slavery* was distasteful to the refined ear, we will not here discuss, but that it existed in the States of the Union is a simple fact. Had the framers of the Constitution put a limit to its extension we question if the signers of this instrument from the Northern and Eastern States would have been, at that time, at all willing inasmuch as they were at that period engaged in the African slave trade, and were turning their own slaves into money by selling them to the South. Nor would the latter have ceded to the Union

[1] James Petigru Carson, *Life, Letters, and Speeches of James Louis Petigru . . .* (Washington, 1920) is the only book-length study of this well-known South Carolinian.

her vast territories in the West to be converted into free states and so limit and crowd that institution into the six Southern States. These framers should have looked ahead and so have avoided all possibility of allowing the more populous North and East to have dictated their construction of the Constitution, and backed up the same by the army and navy and by her vast resources of men and money. Was there any "Justice" when, instead of "insuring domestic Tranquility," the abolitionists of the North and East left no stone unturned to stir up strife among our servants and incite them into insurrection, and subsequently to have marched into Virginia with the avowed purpose of murdering the whites and freeing the slaves, as John Brown and his band attempted? If this is the letter and the spirit of the Constitution then were the Southern States most unwise, to use a mild term, to enter into any such compact. But the struggle had to come sooner or later, for it was impossible that a people so antagonistic as were the Puritans and Cavaliers should live any longer in peace. . . .

Thirty-five years ago the armies of the North, the East, and the West were marching into the South to put down what they were pleased to call rebellion, and to free the negroes, and to enslave the whites by placing the negroes on an equality with their former masters. Their object has been in some degree accomplished and peace restored; but the race problem is not solved and coming generations will have to grapple with an issue which must inevitably come and which astute statesmen would have postponed to some more convenient season. . . .

These negroes taken from the wilds of Africa, cruel and inhuman as was this cursed traffic, had been introduced into the Southern States and had proven a most valuable acquisition to a country which was destined to be the home of indigo, rice, cotton, and sugar in the provinces of Carolina and Georgia, and subsequently in the Southern States. It is interesting to speculate on what would have been the condition of the country had this slave labor not have been introduced. In many respects it would have been far better for the future wealth of the Southern States. That vast area of the country, extending from the Atlantic to the Mississippi and beyond, would not have been denuded of its valuable forests of live oak, pine, walnut, etc., which at the present time would have been of inestimable value. Each acre of these many millions clothed in their valuable timbers, would have been worth (apart from the tide water swamp lands of Carolina and Georgia, where the cultivation of rice rendered them very valuable, and where the timber was not so, and the alluvial lands of the Mississippi and other large rivers of the West, the great cotton region) at least three or four times more than their present value.

Cast your eye over the above named states and see in the red clay fields, washed and gullied, how destructive was slave labor to their future wealth; for it was the custom to cultivate these lands in cotton and corn till worn out and then abandon them, and clear up fresh acres. Fertilizers were not applied as long as new forests could be reached and the fine timber felled and burned on the ground on which it lay. Where a planter could take his labor with him he was always at home, and so were fields cultivated in a great degree to the exclusion of that inestimable blessing, a love of home. This was not the case with the rice plantations. The work was too stupendous, and the machinery too expensive to be abandoned, and the lands too rich to be exhausted. And so the homes on the banks of these rivers were in a great many cases handed down from one generation to another, and the negroes thereon became much attached to the soil on which they had so long lived. But their homes in turn, where peace and prosperity for so many generations walked hand in hand, have fallen into decay; handsome residences burned or dilapidated, valuable mills out of gear and mostly in the hands of negro tenants, who cultivate the soil a la Congo. . . . Thus has the "negro question" become one of great magnitude.

I would greatly deplore the day when the negroes of the olden times should conclude to remove to that dark continent from which they came. Such have wound themselves around the best feelings of those of our race who knew them so intimately and appreciate them so thoroughly. Both [races] of those [old days] are fast passing away and it would be infinitely better that the old time negro should be laid to rest beneath the earth which he tilled so faithfully under the superintendence of what our Northern friends are pleased to call his "cruel task-master". . . .

If the General Government is wise it will begin, even now, to cast about for a home for the negro. Not that I would see him forced away against his will, but that a home be carefully selected where he can enjoy the advantages of a climate suitable to his peculiar constitution and temperament, and where he can work out his own salvation by showing himself capable of self government. It is simply cruel to tempt him to emigrate to Liberia, whose climate is fatal to health and civilization. No portion of the United States could be set apart, simply because the white inhabitants would never permit it and because in a few years there would not be standing room for this race producing people. No, the negro must return to the home of his fathers, not as the prodigal son, but as one who had been wrested from his native forests and for an avaricious purpose sold into slavery, but as a civilized being, into whose heart had been planted the seeds of Christianity, which will, in God's good time, shed the light of the Cross over benighted Africa. This then is the mission of the ex-slaves of the South. To lure them on to Liberia is unwise, unjust, and cruel. Up the Congo river to some region near Victoria Niganza, where a climate similar to that of the low countries of the Southern States, where the soil is fertile and where there are thousands of miles of navigable water courses, is the destined home of the negro. There he will be free from the aggressive peril of the white man, and there prove himself a man. But the home must be prepared for him, for he never will be able to do for his race what the Anglo Saxon did in America. Had the negro landed here he would have soon been annihilated by the Indians. Appropriations will have to be made for his deportation, and philanthropy blaze out for him a path in the wilderness and point out to him the way he should go. He cannot and should not expect to antagonize the white race and reap the reward of all the hardships which they have encountered. The hour they felt themselves to be wards of the nation that hour was their own civilization retarded, perhaps for centuries.

There are some birds which do not build nests for themselves, but occupy those which have been abandoned; let the negro avoid, if he can, this lack of energy and make the dark Continent, old in the history of the world, new in that civilization which he was destined to bring back with him from the Western hemisphere. The negro can never expect to occupy any higher place than he now holds in the United States. He is held in far greater esteem at the South than in the North and West, but the color line is distinctly marked—"thus far shalt thou go, but no further"—and if he is wise he will ponder those things. . . .

It was during the Civil War that Charleston was swept by a most disastrous fire which broke out in the northeastern portion of the City and burned through to the southwestern limits. An immense amount of property was destroyed, and many old landmarks annihilated. The old historic colonial residence of the Pinckneys was consumed. It was here that the mother of Generals Charles Cotesworth and Thomas Pinckney lived. She was Eliza Lucas, a very remarkable woman, who before her marriage to Charles Pinckney introduced indigo and silk into the province of Carolina. She had three silk gowns made, one of which is in Charleston at the present time.[2] I have often heard my grandmother speak of her, but I was too young and heedless to note with accuracy all that was told me.

The Izard residence on West Broad Street was also burned. It was here that my Cousin Tom Pinckney lived, the son of General Thomas Pinckney.[3] I called him "Cousin" as his father General Pinckney married the daughter of Jacob and Rebecca Motte, Elizabeth, who died in England when General Pinckney was Minister to the Court of St. James. General Pinckney, on his return to Carolina married Mrs. Middleton, the widow of a young Englishman who came over to help the American cause. She was also a daughter of Jacob and Rebecca Motte, Frances Motte. I remember her quite well, and would see her home nearly every evening when she took tea with her sister, my grandmother Alston.

Many public buildings were destroyed: the old Circular Church on Meeting Street, the Mechanic Institute, also on Meeting Street, where the Convention for nominating a presidential candidate in 1860 was held and which adjourned without having accomplished its object. . . .[4] I cannot enumerate the prominent buildings which were burned. The Roman Catholic Cathedral and the Saint Cecelia's Hall fell victims to the cruel flames. At the latter, the Saint Cecelia balls were given when only the elite were received, and the Jockey Club Ball in February during the races. Colonel Tom Pinckney was the President of the Jockey Club. Among his many accomplishments

---

[2] Mrs. St. Julien Ravenel, *Eliza Lucas Pinckney* (New York, 1896). Although Mrs. Pinckney is generally credited with the introduction of indigo, attempts at silk-raising had been made before her time. See Wallace, *South Carolina: A Short History*, pp. 189-91.

[3] *Dictionary of American Biography*, XIV, 617-18.

[4] Francis B. Simkins and Robert H. Moody, *South Carolina During Reconstruction* (Chapel Hill, N.C., 1932), pp. 5 and 314.

singing was not prominent, but at the sumptuous supper after the ball he was always called upon for a song, and "The high mettled racer" invariably followed, which was always received with applause, not from the artistic rendition, but on account of the esteem for the man. . . .[5]

To give some idea of the appearance of things in Charleston when peace was declared by the surrender of Lee, and previous to that hell on earth called Reconstruction, I will here give you a bird's eye view of the old King Street home which, of course, had been abandoned by the family during the long bombardment of the enemy. I left the up-country and made a visit to the old city and home of my early life. The railroads were destroyed in many places, and stage coaches used to connect the broken links; and improvised roads made traveling a rough and tumble affair. My dear Aunt Hesse had just returned to her home; the beautiful chandelier, which had been in place for over 100 years and which could not well be carried off, was, strange to say, uninjured, and the frames of the portraits still clung to the walls. Our meeting was, of course, a sad one, but all had become accustomed to sadness—it was our normal condition—and "from our enemies defend us" was about the only prayer uttered. A little cot in the drawing room was my sleeping place and one can well imagine with what sad feelings I compared the past with the present. Of course the floors were bare, for the beautiful Axminster carpet which had been woven for the room in one piece had been removed, . . . captured by the enemy at Cheraw and cut up for saddle cloths. . . .

As I strolled through the extensive gardens, where huge shells, unexploded, were scattered around and where the rank weeds outranked the beautiful flowers (fit emblems of the existing state of affairs), I keenly felt the immense change which like a pall had spread over the entire country, but in Carolina above the rest. To walk the streets was a melancholy task. The great fire, of which I have written, which swept through the entire City from northeast to southwest,

[5] See [Irving], *South Carolina Jockey Club,* p. 152: "From time immemorial . . . after the cloth is removed . . . everybody . . . is hushed into a profound silence. The President then *takes the lead* . . . with 'The High Mettled Racer'; when no sooner is the last note of this admirable song breathed, than a most unanimous hammering of the tables, and rattling of the glasses, proclaim its termination." On the following page the four stanzas of this stirring song are printed in full.

had destroyed so much valuable property, [which] of course had not been rebuilt. The bare and blackened walls and the green weeds which had sprung up around, presented a strange appearance—a neglected City of the Dead. How many negroes whom I had known came up to shake hands and make kindly remarks, which were, it is useless to say, fully reciprocated. . . .

The bitterness of the North evinced itself by the long but ineffectual attack on Charleston by sea—the defense of which has given to history no more gallant achievement—and the wanton destruction of Columbia by fire. . . .

Always remember that our laboring class were negroes who were not put into the Southern armies, whilst at the North, East, and West this class were whites. This will at once show how unequal was the contest from its incipiency. The Northern Army was composed of all nationalities, the bulk of whom fought for money and not principle. Of course, there were honorable exceptions, but the make up of the armies was vastly different, and so our cities were drained of men, and all industries came to a stand still whilst the North had a chance of getting rid of her surplus population. Even the jails and penitentiaries were emptied of criminals to finish out their terms of service for the subjugation of the South. I remember one or two companies of this material deserted and were stationed near Columbia, South Carolina. One night they robbed General Hampton's residence. The ladies of the family sent for me and told me of the burglary. I went to where they were encamped and strolled around, for I had a strong suspicion that I could locate the theft. I then went to the quarters of the officers and told them that I had strong suspicions that these fellows had robbed Hampton's house. When I left, one of these "soldiers of fortune" followed me all over the city and then had the assurance to join me to endeavor to find out what I came to the camp for. Of course, I threw him off the scent, for I was too old a hunter to be taken in by such cattle. I then felt sure of my game and just before the troops left, the ground under their tents was up turned and, sure enough, the stolen silver, jewelry, etc., were discovered, identified by the family and recovered. In their haste to leave the house, these jail birds dropped on the floor a valuable diamond necklace.

The cities of the North were teeming with an industrious population, bent on making money. Contracts for the materials of war, contracts for feeding and clothing the vast army to be placed in the field made millionaires of men of only moderate means before, and made it an easy matter to send substitutes to the front. And so the old South, with her hallowed associations, lives only in the past, or as Robert Toombs facetiously said, "wore herself out in whipping the Yankees." . . .[6]

And whilst alluding to . . . [the burning of Columbia], let me give a short account of what I saw in connection with the same. I happened to be [away from home] in the neighborhood of Fort Motte, twenty miles below Columbia, in St. Matthews Parish, just before Sherman marched on Columbia. We were occupying a cottage near Millwood, the residence of the Hamptons, some five miles from the City. [Upon hurrying home I found that] Christopher Hampton had removed his sisters to a safe place up the railroad.[7] On the morning that Columbia was attacked I passed through Columbia with my family during the attack as it was most unsafe to have remained longer in the cottage. Having seen the two carriages safely out of reach of the enemy some miles beyond the city, I rode back to the cottage to give some orders about a well ladened wagon of trunks, etc., which was to follow (and which we never saw again, as it was robbed and then burned), directing where the family was to halt for the night. I could not overtake the carriage till dark and then we beheld the burning of Columbia from the high hill on which the house was situated. . . . We were only twelve miles away, and it was wonderful to see how rapidly the city burned, and I question if any other fire had ever spread so rapidly. . . . On the next day we reached Alston on the Broad river and on the morning of the following, crossed over (having abandoned our vehicles) on a dirty train, the railroad bridge being burned behind us, and the pickets of both armies being on each side of the railroad. And so we bade adieu to Columbia, our once happy home. . . .

Amid the accumulation of troubles how well it is that the future is hidden so wisely and so kindly from our view. . . .

After reaching Greenville, I returned to Columbia. The smoke hung in heavy clouds over the ruined city; all was confusion and there was much suffering. I walked to my Aunt's, Mrs. A. P. Hayne,

---

[6] *Dictionary of American Biography,* XVIII, 590-92.

[7] Christopher Hampton was the son of the second Wade Hampton and brother of the third.

a mile or two out of the city, and found that the old Colonel and herself had been pretty roughly treated. Colonel Hayne relied on the fact that his having been a Colonel in the U.S. Army and Aide to General Jackson at the battle of New Orleans, and at the same time being over seventy years of age, would protect him from the rude soldiers of Sherman. But you must remember that they were in Carolina, where every license was permitted, and so the residence was robbed of all that could be carried off, and the poor old Colonel was only cursed when he informed them who he was, and when he refused to give up his valuable watch, was pushed down and robbed. Some very fine old wine which I had stored in his home for my Uncle Charles Alston was all stolen, but the rascals failed to get the best of the old wine, which was secreted where they failed to find it. All was topsy-turvy at my dear Aunt's house—boxes, trunks, etc., were broken open, and plundered.

The next day I walked to Millwood and to the cottage which we had left. The beautiful residence of the former was burned to the ground, only the chimneys and white columns in front were standing. I found my friend, Christopher Hampton, standing in the gardener's house. He had also returned to see what had been left of the home of his fathers. We shook hands but little was said. He then pointed to me a letter which lay open on the table, which I carefully read. It was written in a clear bold hand and signed by Lieutenant Colonel ——— (I do not remember at this late date the name, but I think it was Strong, the Hamptons however do), of the army under General Sherman. The substance of the letter was "that as soon as he had crossed the Congaree he rode to Millwood with a squad of his men to protect the Hampton property but found that the residence had been already fired and was too far consumed to be saved." The letter was addressed to General Wade Hampton of the Confederate army and expressed the deepest regret that the place had been destroyed, and wound up by saying that he had understood that he (General H.) was a keen sportsman and hoped that he would yet meet him in pleasanter fields. No letter could have been more sincere or couched in more friendly terms. Remember that Millwood was five miles below Columbia and consequently that distance out of Sherman's march, thus involving a ten mile ride to save the property. This officer only knew the Hampton family by reputation, and there could be no other construction placed on his visit but that he was aware that the residence had been on the list of those destined to be destroyed.

A very faithful servant of mine told me that he was present when the house was fired, and that one of the soldiers was playing on the piano whilst the fire was consuming the building. To make assurance doubly sure all the buildings on one side of the road were burned so as to insure that that of the Hamptons did not escape. It was very sad to see the total loss of this time honored and hospitable abode.

A quarter of a mile farther on was the cottage where I had resided only a few days before. It was pretty thoroughly robbed but not burned, as the servant above alluded to, Richmond, said to the soldiers that it belonged to him and protested against its destruction and that his master's furniture, etc., etc., had been left in his care. Many articles of value he had buried in various places, but trunks and boxes had been broken open and valuables stolen—in rifling one of which, an old gold watch which had belonged to my great grandmother, Mrs. Rebecca Motte, was thrown out and escaped the hungry eyes of these well trained soldiers of the Union, when another of my servants put his foot on it and so concealed it till he could put it in his pocket. When the old relic of the past—which had noted the time of day at Fort Motte when Marion's men captured the British forces by first firing the building and then saving same from destruction—began to tick so loudly . . . Billy went to bed, saying he was sick, in order to escape the keen ears of these watch-takers. I need not say that the watch and old wines, etc., which these oppressed people of mine had saved, were promptly handed me on my return, on this tour of inspection.[8] . . . I was much pleased when C. F. Hampton that day said to me, "Alston, I thought our servants were most faithful, but yours are more so". . . .

On the next day I walked into Columbia to see the wreck of a once lovely little city. The smoldering fires and forest of tall chimneys, looming up about the same, told of the desolated homes of the mothers, wives, and children of those who in Virginia and the West were fighting to protect these same now devastated firesides. Many sad tales of woe greeted our ears (C. F. Hampton and self), as we moved through the ruins. The finest residence in the city, that of Mrs. Hampton, then owned by General John S. Preston, was saved

[8] The watch which Billy saved is now in possession of Mr. Alston's granddaughter, Mary Alston Read Simms.

from destruction by the inmates of the Convent [which occupied the building] . . .

One of the saddest cases was the burning of the dwelling of Dr. Robert Gibbes, Senior, who was much esteemed in the community in which he had so long resided, and who had gathered around him quite a collection of works of art, paintings, etc., all of which he had carefuly secreted in his residence near Main Street, before the brigade of burners crossed the Congaree, armed with fire balls, which they ignited and pitched into the buildings as they passed along. The Doctor's home was repeatedly fired and as often extinguished by him in the vain effort to save what was so valuable to him. . . .[9]

I asked the Misses Hampton and also General Hampton why the letter which I have referred to was not produced and so have settled, for all time, the question as to "who burned Columbia?" and was told that unfortunately that valuable letter had been lost. There are of course, many now living who witnessed the mode in which the city was fired; but that letter which I so carefully read, proved conclusively that it was premeditated. . . .

The railroad was burned from Columbia to Newberry and so I had to ride on a wagon minus springs or body to reach the burned city, but on my return a gentleman offered me a seat in his carriage to Greenville. For twenty miles of the route everything had been destroyed save the earth and the timber thereon. No life was visible save the buzzards feeding on the dead horses, cattle, and hogs which lay along the road side. Not a bushel of corn, or handful of forage left; farm houses all destroyed and not even the crowing of a cock could be heard to tell that some habitation was near at hand; only the chimneys pointed out where they had been. Broken down vehicles strewed the way, and among them, strange to say, I saw a buggy of mine that I had given a very high price for; it was nearly new and only an axle a little bent prevented its being removed and so recovered. As the river was too high to cross the carriages and horses over, I had to abandon my companion and passed the night in walking to where I could reach the railroad some thirty miles [away]. . . .

---

[9] A description of this collection may be found in Arney R. Childs, *Robert Wilson Gibbes* ("University of South Carolina Bulletin," No. 210 [Columbia, n. d.]), pp. 14 and 28. In a letter from Dr. Gibbes to his son written shortly after the burning of Columbia the story of the burning of his home is recounted. See *ibid.*, pp. 32-33.

The fearful ordeal which the south had to endure at the hands of the victorious North during the years of what was called reconstruction is burned on the heart of every man and woman of the South, and should be on every stone under which they lie. . . .

The state legislatures were *the* features of the period. Barnum, with all his ingenuity and talent for collecting trained animals, would have been a grim failure besides one of these menageries. The beautiful State House in Columbia, South Carolina, designed by [John R. Niernsee] was oft times a scene worthy of Hogarth. Saturate your handkerchief with cologne and walk up the beautiful marble steps, stand at the door where a whiff of fresh air can reach you, and look in upon this motley body of legislators—white, black, and all the various intermixtures. The speaker of the House is the *honorable* Franklin J. Moses, who owns the old Hampton residence, the handsomest in Columbia, and only saved from Sherman's torch by having been occupied by the nuns when the City was fired. This Moses was afterwards Governor of Carolina and has served various terms in many penitentiaries at the North.[10] It was this same Moses who, when Speaker, lost $1,000 at a horse race. The negro member who won the money knew full well how slim were the chances of getting his money, so he adroitly moved, at the end of the session, that the thanks of the House be offered to the Speaker, and a thousand dollars in addition, for his uniform politeness and fairness. It was seconded and carried, and so the Speaker pocketed the politeness; and the darkey, the money.

Well—these halls and committee rooms were sumptuously furnished by those members who stole untold thousands from the State. Axminster carpets and beautiful curtains and chandeliers—even the spittoons cost over ten dollars each—all to be trampled under foot by these swine. Vulgarity and rascality ruled the house. It was all this, and what no decent pen could trace, which alienated the negro from his former owner. . . .[11]

The newspapers tell us that the South is improving, and so she is in some sections; but on the coast region of Carolina and Georgia and along the Gulf, this once highly cultured and cultivated region is

[10] Simkins and Woody, *South Carolina During Reconstruction,* pp. 126, 127, 545.

[11] *Ibid.,* pp. 120 ff.

fast retrograding; and in many sections of those alluvial lands, the tall, rank weeds, the alligator, and the negro are contending for the mastery, and here it would be safe to bet one thousand to one against the latter. . . .

After the wreck which the civil war caused it is difficult to realize that they who lived before and those who survived were the same; and I have often felt that death and not life was the boon to be craved. The fragments of families as they float along in the great whirlpool which disrupted them seem to cling together for protection, but the spirit which animated them is crushed and broken; and so do we reach back into the past for those joys which will ne'er come again. . . . All those sweet associations rendered hallowed by the dear ones who have passed away, and all the countless homes where peace and happiness loved to dwell, live only in the memories of those who survive. The deserted or burned dwellings tell the sad tale of ruthless war, of united families scattered to the four corners of the earth, of ancient burial grounds, surrounded by the oaks of centuries, where gentle hands did tend in tearful love, but now covered over with tall grasses, or only such wild flowers which loving Nature had entwined around the tombs of those who had once bowed their heads to Nature's God. But amid all of these surroundings there is some happiness left. . . .

How small things cling to us when those of far more importance pass from our recollection; and this fact recalls a dream I had quite recently, which may explain to those who believe in dreams why even minute occurrences are on record. I was in a ball room filled with lovely women, one of whom was patiently and carefully winding a fine thread on a card. I watched her curiously, and not being able to explain to myself her monotonous occupation, I asked a lady who was near me what it meant. "Why that is the 'thread of life'—not that which we have ever learned to believe could be so easily broken, and so sever us from the cares and joys of this life; but on the thread which she is so slowly and carefully winding is recorded every thought and act of our lives." The dream was so vivid that I was awakened and I pondered over the significance of it. "Seeming trifles do make up the sum and substance of our lives," it is asserted, and if this be true "then should we not despise the day of small things." . . .

But I am ever and anon getting ahead of my simple story. Will any one take the trouble to read it? I ween not, the manuscript is difficult, for which I am not now responsible, and the long road over which I have traveled and the "jotting down" of an every-day life can hold but little interest in this age of rapid transit, and phenomenal inventions and scientific research.

When I made the promise to record some facts of family interest, I little dreamed I would be led to retrace so many joyful or weary steps that mark the mile stones in a man's long pilgrimage. But I have made a beginning and unless I hasten on, the sunset of this life may overtake me and so I call a halt for weal or for woe, to this home-spun tale.

Genealogical Table

NOTE: The material in this table is drawn from several sources including Elizabeth Deas Allston, *The Allstons and Alstons of Waccamaw;* a number of issues of the *South Carolina Historical and Genealogical Magazine;* and Genealogical Notes compiled by Motte Alston Read and given by his sister, Mary Alston Read Simms to the South Carolina Historical Society. Miss Helen G. McCormack very kindly did the gleaning of this last named material. The family burial plot in Trinity Churchyard, Columbia, South Carolina, supplied some needed information.

The chart reads from right to left, following the numbered names and is not complete in detail but is limited chiefly to the people appearing in the book.

1. John Alston (or Allston), Emigrant, of St. John's b. 1666 m. Mrs. Elizabeth Harris	Six children, including *John,* II (2.) *William* (3.)
2. John Allston, II b. *ca.* 1696 d. 1750 m. 2. Sarah Belin	Five children, including William ("Gentleman William," who retained the double *l,* lived at Brookgreen and was the father of Washington Allston)
3. William Allston, I b. 1698 d. 1743 m. Esther Labrosse (or LaBruce) de Marboeuf	Eleven children, including *Joseph* of The Oaks (4.)
4. Joseph Allston b. 1732 m. Charlotte Rothmaler	Six children, including *William,* ("King William," who dropped one *l* from his name) (5.)

5. William Alston of Clifton b. 1757 d. 1839 m. 1. 1777 Mary Ashe	Maria b. 1778 m. Sir John Nesbit Joseph (Governor) b. 1779 d. 1812 m. Theodosia Burr John Ashe b. 1780 d. 1812 m. Sarah McPherson William Algernon b. 1782 d. 1860 m. Mrs. Mary Allston Young (nine children including John Ashe Alston II) Charlotte
m. 2. 1791 Mary Brewton Motte b. 1769 d. 1838	Rebecca m. Robert Y. Hayne *Thomas Pinckney* (6.) Charles m. Emma Pringle Jacob Motte b. 1797 d. 1818 Elizabeth m. A. P. Hayne Mary Motte ("Hesse") m. William Bull Pringle—14 children
6. Thomas Pinckney Alston b. 1795 d. 1861 m. 1. 1820 Jane Ladson Smith b. 1800 d. 1823	*Jacob Motte* (author of these recollections) (7.)
m. 2. 1825 Susan Smith b. 1805 d. 1884	Charles b. 1826 d. 1869 m. Washington Dunkin Mary Brewton b. 1827 m. J. J. Waring William b. 1829 Susan Elizabeth b. 1830 m. Cleland Huger Thomas Pinckney b. 1832 d. 1864 John Rutledge b. 1835 Rebecca and Jane b. 1838 Jane d. 1842 Elizabeth Laura b. 1841 d. 1843 Jane Ladson b. 1843 d. 1878
7. Jacob Motte Alston b. 1821 d. 1909 m. 1848 Mary Ann Fitzsimons b. 1830 d. 1866	Thomas Pinckney b. 1849 d. 1868 Ellen b. 1850 m. John Cooper Jane Ladson b. 1852 m. William Melvin Read d. 1920 Anna Hampton b. 1853 m. George Garvin d. 1878 Mary Motte b. 1855 d. 1911 Catherine Fitzsimons b. 1857 m. H. H. Steiner Pauline Fitzsimons b. 1859 d. 1861 ("Lily") Hesse Pringle b. 1861 m. R. S. Trapier Jacob Motte b. 1863 d. 1885

Index

Abolitionists, 130
Adams, Jasper, 21, 22, 23, 24, 25
All Saints Church and Parish, xxxvii, 48, 59, 60, 124
Allston, Aaron Burr, xxxviii, 8, 38
Allston, John (the emigrant) xxxvii, 4, 51
Allston, John E., xvii
Allston, Joseph, Governor, xxxviii, 8, 17, 39, 110
Allston, Mrs. Joseph. *See* Burr, Theodosia
Allston, Washington, xxxix, 4 106, 108
Allston, William (First), xxxvii, 4
Alston, Anna, 108
Alston, Charles (uncle of J. M. A.), 25, 28, 37, 38, 109, 137
Alston, Mrs. Charles. *See* Pringle, Emma
Alston, Charles (half-brother of J. M. A.), 15, 126
Alston, Charlotte, 108
Alston, Elizabeth (Mrs. Arthur P. Hayne), 116, 136
Alston, Hesse (Mrs. Richard S, Trapier, dau. of J. M. A.), xl
Alston, J. Motte (uncle of J. M. A.), 25, 26, 27
Alston, Mrs. J. Motte. *See* Fitzsimons, Mary Ann
Alston, Jane Ladson (Mrs. William M. Read), xxxviii, 3
Alston, John Ashe (uncle of J. M. A.), 110
Alston John Ashe (cousin of J. M. A.), 51, 106, 107, 124
Alston, John Rutledge (brother of J. M. A.), 82
Alston, Maria (Lady Nesbit), 19, 19n., 33
Alston, Mary Motte ("Hesse," Mrs. William Bull Pringle, aunt of J. M. A.), 8, 9, 37, 134
Alston, Mary (dau. of J. M. A.), xl
Alston, Sally (Mrs. John Izard Middleton), 110
Alston, T. Pinckney (father of J. M. A.), 11,19, 20, 21, 24, 25, 26, 27, 29, 32, 35, 36, 37, 50, 51, 60, 71, 73, 93, 102, 103, 107, 112
Alston, Mrs. T. Pinckney. *See* Smith, Jane Ladson; Smith, Susan
Alston, Thomas (uncle of J. M. A.), 20, 25, 37, 49
Alston, Thomas Pinckney (son of J. M. A), 118
Alston, William Algernon (uncle of J.M. A.) 51, 106, 107, 108
Alston, William of Clifton (grandfather of J. M. A.), xxxiv, xxxvii, xxxviii, xxxix, 4, 6, 10, 12, 13, 16, 20, 25, 26, 27, 37, 39, 49, 50, 67
Anderson Robert, 71

Bear hunt, 98-99
Belmont, August, 128
Boats between Georgetown and Charleston: "Martha Pyatt," 29; "Little Jack," 29; "Nina," 115, 122
Bonaparte, Charles, 11-12
Brewton, Miles, 14, 17
Brewton-Alston-Pringle House (27 Church St., Charleston), xvii, 7, 14, 15, 16, 17, 134
Brewton, Rebecca (Mrs. Jacob Motte), xxxviii, 4, 5, 14, 15, 26, 133, 138
Brewton, Robert, 14

Brown, John, 130
Buck, Henry, 125
Burr, Aaron, 9, 17
Burr, Theodosia (Mrs. Joseph Allston), xxxvii, 8, 9, 10, 17, 110

Castle Pinckney, 115
Chamche, President John, 35
Charleston College, 21, 28
Charleston earthquake 1886, 19
Charleston fire, 133, 134-135, 186
Clarke, W. O., 52, 53, 54, 55
Clinch, General, 71
Coates (Cotes), Christopher, 30, 31, 32
Columbia, burning of, 135, 136, 139, 140
Cooking: rice, xl, 78-79; fish, 94
Cooper, James Fenimore, 111, 112
Cotton land, value of, xxxv, 20

Daggett, Tom, 125
Davis, Bishop Thomas F., 56, 121
Deas, Elizabeth (Mrs. John E. Allston), xxxix
Debordieu Island, 5, 5n., 7, 8, 18, 25, 37, 58, 106, 107, 122, 124
Deer hunting: "still hunting," 83; deer drive, 84, 98
Democratic Conventions of 1860, 128, 133
Dickens, Charles, 38
Douglas, Stephen, 128
Duck hunting: Chesapeake Bay, 79; Waccamaw Neck, 79-82, 86
Duelling, 21

Flagg, Arthur, 26, 105
Fishing: favorable conditions for, 87-88; equipment for, 88; bream 88-90; perch, 90; use of bob, spoon, spinner, 90-91; bass, 91; on Tow River, N.C., 100, 101
Fitzsimons, Ann (Mrs. Wade Hampton, Second), 114
Fitzsimons, Mary Ann (Mrs. J. Motte Alston), xxxviii, 65, 71, 72, 73, 103, 106, 118, 125
Fitzsimons, Colonel Paul, 114
Fitzsimons, Mrs. Paul, 110 112
Fort Moultrie, 115, 116, 117
Fort Sumter, 38, 115
Fraser, Charles, 7, 106
Fraser, Fanny, 106

Georgetown, S.C., 5, 6, 7, 102
Gibbes, Dr. Robert W., 139
Glennie, Reverend Alexander, 48, 59, 60, 86, 121
Guns: Joe Manton, 11; Westly Richards, 53

Hamilton, Governor James, 33
Hammond, Governor James H., 111
Hampton, The Misses, 139
Hampton, Christopher, 136, 137, 138
Hampton, General Wade (First), 114
Hampton, Colonel Wade (Second), 100, 114
Hampton, Mrs. Wade (Second). *See* Fitzsimons, Ann
Hampton, General Wade (Third), 33, 100, 114, 126, 135, 137, 139
Hampton, Mrs. Wade (Third). *See* Preston, Margaret
Hatch, General J. P., 15
Hayne, Arthur P., 39, 116, 137
Hayne, Mrs. Arthur P. *See* Alston, Elizabeth
Hayne, Robert Y., 21
Horses: Crusader, 19; marsh tackeys, 28, 87; Nick of the Woods, 53, 80
"Hot and Hot Fish Club," 60, 61, 106
Huntington, Archer M., xxxix

Jayhawkers, 82
Jockey Club: 20, 67; ball, 19, 133-134

Ka-a (summer home of T. Pinckney Alston), 71, 72, 96, 103, 118, 122
Kershaw and Lewis (later Kershaw, Lewis and Robertson, rice factors), 67
King's Highway (Waccamaw Neck), xxxix
Kirton, Sam (overseer), 109

La Fayette: in Charleston (1825), 17, 18
Lesesne, Henry D., 52
Longstreet, Mrs., 110
Lucas, Eliza (Mrs. Charles Pinckney), 133

Manigault, Mr., 29
Manning, Governor John L., 126
Marboeuf de Labrosse (LaBruce), Esther (Mrs. William Allston, First), xxxvii
Marion, Francis, 4n., 17, 112
Meyers family, 8
Middleton, Arthur, 4
Middleton, Henry, 110
Middleton, John Izard, 110
Middleton, Mrs. John Izard. *See* Alston, Sally
"Millwood," home of Colonel Wade Hampton, 114, 137-38
Moses, Franklin J., 140
Motte, Elizabeth (Mrs. Thomas Pinckney), 133
Motte, Frances (Mrs. John Middleton, afterwards Mrs. Thomas Pinckney), 17, 133
Motte, Jacob, 133
Motte, Mrs. Jacob. *See* Brewton, Rebecca
Motte, Mary Brewton (Mrs. William Alston, grandmother of J. M. A.), xxxviii, 4, 7, 8, 10, 13, 16, 17, 21, 24, 25, 26, 27, 29, 32, 35, 36, 37, 133

Nesbit, Lady. *See* Alston, Maria
Niernsee, John R., 140
Nullification Controversy, 21

Overseer: pay of, 56, 109; responsibility of, 62, 63; brutality of, 109-110

Partridge shooting, 96, 97
Pawley's Island, 57, 58, 65, 66, 68, 122
PeeDee Club, 34
Petigru, James L., 24, 129
Petigru, Thomas, 24
Pierpont, John, 25, 25n.
Pinckney, Chief Justice Charles, 115
Pinckney, Mrs. Charles. *See* Lucas, Eliza
Pinckney, Charles Cotesworth, 115, 133
Pinckney, Thomas (First), 5, 115, 133
Pinckney, Thomas (Second), 5, 133
Plantations, Waccamaw Neck: Clifton, xxxiv, xxxviii, xxxix, 4, 7, 10, 25, 47; The Oaks, xxxviii, 110; Fairfield, xxxix, 7, 10, 12, 21, 25, 42, 45, 47; Brookgreen, xxxix 45; Prospect Hill, 7; Weehawka, 10, 27, 39, 47, 56, 57, 58, 62, 66, 110; Maryetta, 11, 28, 37, 38; Strawberry Hill, 20, 37, 106; Bellefield, 37; True Blue, 39, 56, 57, 58, 62, 66, 85, 102, 110, 118, 122; Hagley, 47, 56, 110; Woodbourne, 57, 64, 66, 68, 69, 93, 104, 108, 110, 118, 120, 123, 124, 125; Rose Hill, 108; Bannockburn, 110; Laurel Hill, 125
Poinsett, Joel R., 105
Preston, John S., 114
Preston, Margaret (Mrs. Wade Hampton, Third), 114
Preston, William C., 114
Pringle, Emma (Mrs. Charles Alston), 110
Pringle, John Julius, 105, 110
Pringle, Mrs. William B. *See* Alston, Mary Motte

Race horses: Comet, 12; Gallatin, 12; Black Maria, 12; Shark, 12; Symmetry, 12; Bertrand, 19, 20; Aratus, 19; Creeping Kate, 19; Monarch, 114; Sovereign, 114
Rail (called also coot, lesser coot), 78
Rawdon, Lord, 15
Read, Motte Alston, xxxiii, 3
Read, Mrs. William M. *See* Alston, Jane Ladson
Railroad travel, 113-14
Read, William Melvin, xxxviii, 3
Reynolds, Sir Joshua, 17

INDEX

Rice birds (called also bob-o-link, reed-bird, May bird), 76-77, 78
Rice culture: yield, 6; introduction of, 41; mode of cultivation of, in South Carolina, 42-43; in Texas and Louisiana, 41-42; rice mills, 42, 45; preparation of land for, 58-59, 119; unusual crops, 62, 63, 64, 65; crop losses in, 69; final returns of, 127
Robertson, Alexander, 16, 67, 68
Robertson and Blacklock, rice factors, 67
Rutledge, John, 112

Sargent, John Singer, 7
Sea voyage, Charleston to Baltimore (1836), 32
Secession: inadvisable, 128; constitutional, 128, 129; outcome of peaceful secession, 129; Ordinance of Secession, 129
Scott, Sir Walter, 111
Simms, William Gilmore, 111, 112
Singleton, "Old," 85, 86
Slavery: number of slaves owned by Alstons, 6, 47; supplies for slaves, 10, 46; livery of Alston house servants, 12; crime and, 46, 61, 62; rice plantation tasks, 46; religious instruction of slaves, 47; mental development of slaves, 48; condition of slaves on arrival, 49; family ownership of slaves, 56; hiring out of slaves, 126; as a cause of war, 129; civilizing influence of, 130; extension of, into west, 130; adverse effects of, 131; future home needed for emancipated slaves, 132; Liberia unsuited for emancipated slaves, 132
Slaves: Billy, xxxvii, 66, 68, 138; Richmond, xxxiv, 118, 119, 123; Robert, xxxix; Carolina, 8; Thomas Turner, 10, 12; Allard, 15; Scipio, 55, 56; Stephen, 63; Cuffee, 106; Will, 107; William or Cudjo, 108, 109; Caija, 108
Smith, Doctor B. Burgh (uncle of J. M. A.), 22, 26, 63, 106
Smith, Jane Ladson (Mrs. T. Pinckney Alston), xxxviii, 7, 20
Smith, John Rutledge, xxxvii
Smith, Mary (aunt of J. M. A.), 50, 56, 124
Smith, Susan (Mrs. T. Pinckney Alston), 50
Smith, Landgrave Thomas, xxxvii, 41
St. Cecelia Ball, 19
St. Mary's College, Baltimore, Md., xxxvii, 7, 32, 33, 34, 35
St. Michael's Church (Charleston), 17, 18, 19, 27, 115, 123
"Star of the West," 129
Storm of October 1822, 8

The Oaks, graveyard, xxxviii, 39, 40, 40n.
32 Mile House, 13
Toombs, Robert, 136
Trapier, Mrs. Richard S. *See* Alston, Hesse
Tucker, John H., 34

"Uncle Billy," 50, 51

Van Buren, President Martin, 34, 35
Vanderbilt, George, xxxix, 6n.

Ward, J. J., 45, 105
Washington, George, xxxix, 7
Washington, Race Course, 19, 20, 67
Weston, Francis Marion, 110
Weston, Plowden, 47-48, 60, 105, 110, 111, 123
Weston, Mrs. Plowden (maiden name uncertain), 48, 56, 110
"Woodlands," home of Wade Hampton (First), 114
Wren, Christopher, 18